.25

Country Crafts

TIME-LIFE BOOKS

Alexandria, Virginia

Country Crafts

*creative craft
projects, from sewing
to woodworking*

A REBUS BOOK

C O N T E N T S

Painting

Crafting Natural Materials

Working with your hands can be an immense-ly satisfying experience. Craft projects like those featured on the following pages offer an opportunity for personal expression and individual achievement that is particularly welcome in this age of technology. You will find there is pleasure to be had in the entire process—in choosing the materials, in settling on a particular color or design, in doing the work itself, and, finally, in enjoy-ing the finished piece. Moreover, if you are on a tight decorating budget, learning a craft may allow you to copy antique pieces, such as grain-painted boxes or Pennsylvania-German hand towels, which you might not otherwise be able to afford. Indeed, virtually all the crafts in this book, represented by such varied projects as a primitive hooked rug, a twig picture frame, and a log cabin doll quilt, take their inspiration from the past, recall-ing America's rich artistic heritage.

Designed to appeal to everyone from beginners to experienced craftspeople, the twenty-eight projects on the following pages involve sewing, embroidery, rugmaking, working with paper, painting, woodworking, and flower crafting. Even if you have never sewn a stitch or held a paintbrush, you should be able to find a project that suits your level of expertise. And, in learning many of these crafts, such as embroidery and rug-hooking, you can try a practice piece to see if you enjoy a particular technique.

For the best results, it is important to read the directions completely before beginning a project. Each craft features a section called Important Information that offers useful background on materials, equipment, and procedures. Following the Important Information section are step-by-step directions, which are keyed to helpful illustrations, diagrams, charts, and patterns. For your convenience, all but one of the patterns in the book are full size, so you will not have to spend time enlarging them.

Throughout the book you will also find practical information on such topics as selecting paints and brushes, dyeing fabric, and drying flowers. While nearly all the materials you will need for the projects are available at crafts and hardware stores, or at sewing, needlework, or florist shops, you can also consult the yellow pages of your telephone book for additional resources. Be sure to buy quality materials and equipment.

As you gain confidence and develop your skills by doing these projects, you may want to adapt the specified techniques, colors, and designs to your own taste. Once you have made the game board on page 134, for example, you could copy one of the colorful antique boards on pages 138-139. But whether you choose to experiment or not, it is important that you get started. While craft projects can be time consuming, you will soon realize that the rewards—and the unique pieces that result—are well worth the effort.

Sewing

*easy projects for
needle and thread*

Of all the needlecrafts, sewing is perhaps the most versatile. Fabric and thread can be combined to make an almost limitless variety of accessories and toys, and you need not be an accomplished seamstress to explore the possibilities. There are several projects in this chapter that would suit a beginner: a yo-yo coverlet that requires no machine stitching, a set of small fabric-covered sewing boxes also produced by hand, and some fast-to-sew pillow shams stitched from purchased napkins so that no pattern is necessary.

There are also a number of projects to make for children, including three stuffed toys—a floppy frog bean bag, a topsy-turvy doll, and a handsome cat pieced from crazy patchwork—as well as a colorful log cabin doll quilt. While some require purchasing a few simple materials, most can be created by merely turning to your scrap basket or by selecting colorful remnants at your local fabric shop.

Sewing frog bean bags from easy-to-cut patterns is a simple project that can be done by hand or machine (see pages 44-47).

Victorian Sewing Boxes

In Victorian times, it was customary for women to keep their embroidery tools in a small sewing box that could be carried easily from room to room. Patterns for making fabric-covered sewing boxes like those shown here were published in late-19th-century ladies' magazines. Very possibly, such colorful ribbon-trimmed boxes were made to be sold at the "fancy fairs" or bazaars that were commonly held to raise money for charitable causes. The boxes can make distinctive Christmas tree ornaments or pretty packaging for small gifts.

◆ IMPORTANT INFORMATION

Each box is made from three identical cardboard sections; the box opens when the pointed ends are gently pressed together. The sections are covered individually with fabric. Although you can use any medium-weight fabric, chintz, velveteen, moiré, or antique satin will lend the boxes a particularly Victorian look. Full-size patterns are given for three box sizes: 8½ inches, 6⅝ inches, and 5½ inches long. Stitch all seams with a ¼-inch seam allowance.

◆ MATERIALS AND EQUIPMENT

For each box:
1 piece medium-weight fabric, 10 x 17
   inches (for outer covering)
1 piece medium-weight fabric, 10 x 17
   inches (for lining)
Lightweight cardboard
1 ball pearl cotton or 1 skein 6-strand
   embroidery floss

Ribbon and fabric flowers (optional)
Thread
Tracing paper
Scissors
Sewing needle
Darning needle
Dressmaker's pins

◆ DIRECTIONS

1. *Making the pattern:* Using a pencil, trace a Sewing Box Pattern on page 13 in the size of your choice onto the tracing paper and cut out.

2. *Making the cardboard sections:* Place the paper pattern on the cardboard, draw around it, and cut out along the line. Repeat twice to make three cardboard sections.

3. *Cutting the fabric and lining:* If your outer fabric does not have a one-way design or dominant motif, place it with the wrong side up on a worktable. With the wrong side up, lay the lining fabric over it. Place a cardboard section on the fabric layers and draw a line around it ¼ inch outside the pattern to make a seam allowance. Pin through both layers within the marked line and cut on the line. Mark one edge with an X to be the top of the section. Repeat twice to make three outer covering pieces and three lining pieces.

4. *Positioning the fabric design:* If your outer fabric has a one-way design or dominant motif, follow Step 3, but cut the lining pieces only. After cutting the lining pieces, place the fabric for the outer covering on the worktable with the right side up. Using a lining piece as a placement pattern, lay it over the outer fabric with the wrong side up and the straight grain aligned, adjusting it until you like the way the fabric design works with the shape. Pin the lining piece to the outer fabric and cut around the edge. Mark one edge with an X to be the top of the section. Repeat twice to make three outer covering pieces.

5. *Covering the cardboard sections:* Stitch along the top edge of one lining and outer covering piece. Trim the seam to ⅛ inch. On the lining only, press ¼ inch to the wrong side along the raw edge. Turn the pieces right side out and press the seamed edge. Slide a cardboard section between the lining and the outer covering, keeping the seam allowance on the lining side of the cardboard. Fold the outer fabric over the edge of the cardboard and pin the lining to it, pulling both fabric pieces taut. On the lining side of the cardboard, slipstitch the two fabric pieces together. Remove the pins. Repeat for the remaining two sections.

6. *Embellishing the top edges:* Using the darning needle and the pearl cotton or three strands of the embroidery floss, embellish the top edge of one of the sections with whipstitching. To whipstitch, hold the section with the outer covering facing you. Starting at the right-hand point of the section, bring the needle up from the lining side ¼ inch from the top edge, slide it over the top edge, and bring it up from the lining side again ¼ inch to the left; continue working to the left, placing the stitches ¼ inch apart (Illustration A-1). When you reach the left-hand point of the section, reverse direction and, working from the left to the right in the same manner, sew through the same holes (Illustration A-2). Repeat for the top edge of one more box section. These two sections will be the box sides; the remaining section will be the box bottom.

7. *Joining the sections:* Using the darning needle and the pearl cotton or three strands of the embroidery floss, join one edge of the box bottom to the lower edge of one box side with weaving stitch. To do weaving stitch, take a small stitch, through the lining only, at one point of the box side to secure the thread. Referring to Illustration B, hold the box side against the box bottom with the outer sides up. Bring the needle up between the two sections and over the edge of the box bottom, piercing the cardboard ⅛ inch from the edge. Pass the needle between the sections again, bring it up over the edge of the box side, and insert it down through the box side ⅛ inch from the edge and ¼ inch from the previous stitch. Repeat, gently shaping the box curve until the other point is reached. Place the remaining box side against the other edge of the box bottom, and weave together in the same manner. Reinforce the ends with a few tiny overcast stitches. Trim with ribbon bows and flowers if desired. ◆

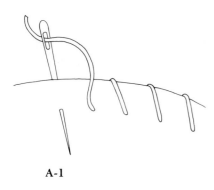

A-1

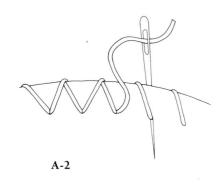

A-2

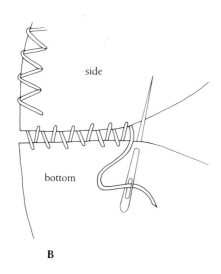

side

bottom

B

SEWING BOX PATTERNS

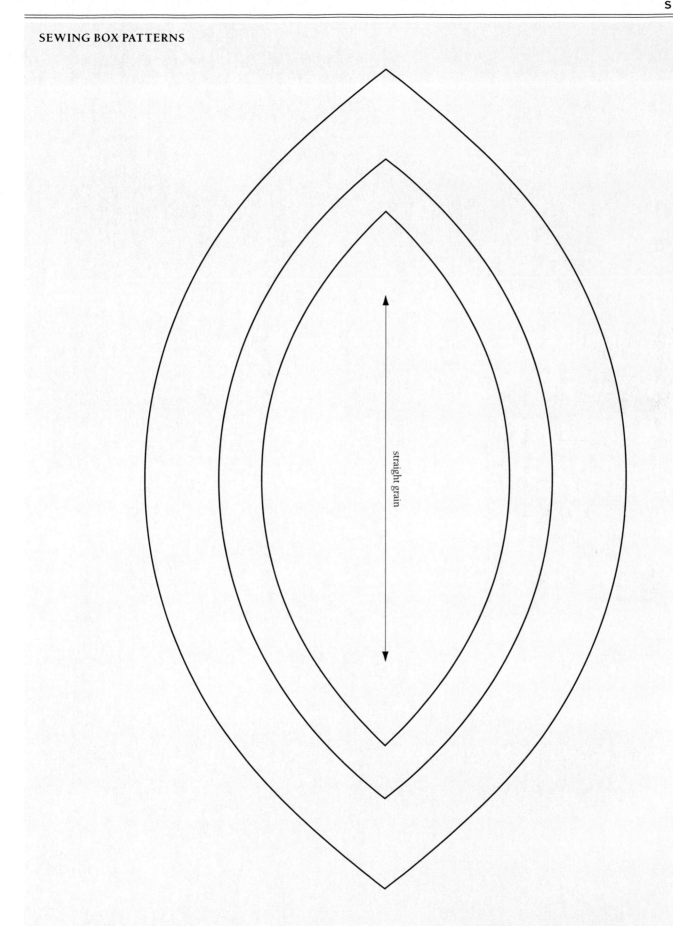

straight grain

PRETTY PINCUSHIONS

Ever since they originated in the 16th century, pincushions have not only been made as utilitarian sewing accessories; they have also been presented as elegant little gifts intended to be enjoyed for their fanciful designs. Pincushions like the 19th- and early-20th-century examples shown here were traditionally pieced from fabric scraps, and often resemble fruits, vegetables, animals, and birds. They might be elaborately embroidered, encrusted with beads, or covered in cotton-thread crochet. In her 1928 book on needlework tools, Gertrude Whiting suggested making "dainty gift cushions" of graduated, scented, pastel-colored hearts. "Each should be edged…with delicate lace and a bit of ribbon of its own hue…," she advised.

As small labors of love, decorative pincushions can still be charming accessories and gifts. Making one is a good way to experiment with a variety of needlework techniques. Let the past inspire you and try replicating a vintage pincushion. Or use the scraps, ribbons, and buttons in your own sewing box to create a new and personal design.

The pincushions shown here date from the 1880s to the 1940s. The crocheted examples at far left were designed to hang on a wall. The Victorian sewing box at near right has a pincushion inside the lid; a bird perches on top.

Napkin Pillow Shams

Cloth napkins are a good fabric choice for pillow shams because they eliminate the need for measuring and cutting pattern pieces. Moreover, many napkins come with a centered pattern or a decorative border that offers the pillow-maker a ready-made design. The shams shown here are made with a back envelope closure so that the case can be easily slipped over a pillow—and just as easily removed for laundering. If desired, the closure can be secured with a button.

◆ IMPORTANT INFORMATION

Choose good-quality cotton or cotton-blend napkins—those shown here are a jacquard cotton—and be sure to preshrink them before you begin sewing. Three matching napkins are used for each pillow sham. Two of them overlap to make the sham back, and the third napkin is used for the sham front. You will need to open the hems on all edges of the front napkin, as well as on the top and bottom edges of the napkins used for the back of the sham; the finished pillow sham will measure the size of one napkin (with the hems opened) less a ½-inch seam allowance.

A tailored hem, or flange, is made by topstitching a 2½-inch border inside the finished edge of the sham. Your pillow should be the same size as the area inside this tailored hem. Ready-made pillows come in many different sizes, but if you cannot find one in the size dictated by the napkins you choose, you can easily make one from polyester stuffing and muslin.

◆ MATERIALS AND EQUIPMENT

For each pillow:
3 cloth napkins, in size desired
1 pillow (see Important Information
   above for size)
Button (optional)

Thread
Scissors
Dressmaker's pins
Dressmaker's chalk
Ruler

◆ DIRECTIONS

1. *Marking the napkin top:* Decide which way you want the napkin pattern to run on your pillow sham. Using a pencil, mark the top edge of each napkin on the wrong side.

2. *Making the sham back:* Remove the hems from the top and bottom edges of two napkins. Press the opened hems. With the wrong side up and the top edge away from you, place one of the two napkins on a worktable. Fold up the left hemmed edge

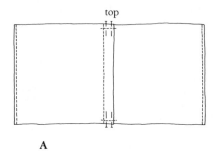

A

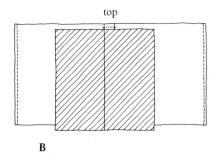

B

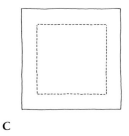

C

1½ inches and press. Topstitch 1¼ inches from the folded edge. This 1½-inch hem will be at the back opening of the sham.

3. *Making the buttonhole (optional):* If the back opening of the sham measures more than 18 inches long, you may want to fasten it with a button. The buttonhole should be made at this time. Find the center of the edge with the 1½-inch hem and mark it for a buttonhole sized to your button. The buttonhole should be perpendicular to the hemmed edge. Make the buttonhole by machine, following the instructions in your operator's manual.

4. *Continuing the sham back:* With the right sides up, place the two napkins for the back on the work surface so that the 1½-inch hem of the first napkin overlaps the left edge of the second napkin. Pin through all the layers and stitch across both ends of the overlap ⅜ inch from the raw edges (Illustration A). Remove the pins and, with the right side up, place the sham back on the worktable in the same position as before.

5. *Making the sham front:* Remove all the hems from the third napkin. Press the opened hems well. With the right sides together, fold the napkin in half to find the center. Using the pencil, mark the center line from top to bottom on the wrong side of the napkin.

6. *Joining the sham front and back:* With the right sides together, place the sham front over the sham back, aligning the center line with the left edge of the lower back napkin (Illustration B). Pin the sham front to the sham back through all the layers around all four edges of the front. Trim the sham back even with the sham front. Stitch a seam with a ½-inch seam allowance along all four edges. Remove the pins and trim the corner seam allowances diagonally. Turn the sham right side out and, using a knitting needle or other blunt-tipped instrument, push out the corners. Press carefully to make the seamed edges sharp.

7. *Making the tailored hem:* With the back facing up, place the sham on the worktable. Pin the back opening closed. Turn the sham over. With the ruler and chalk, measure and mark a line 2½ inches in from the outer edges of the sham. Topstitch along this marked line (Illustration C). Remove the pins from the back opening. Sew on the button, if appropriate. Press the sham. Insert the pillow through the back opening. ◆

THE CRAFTY BUTTON

Much more than utilitarian fasteners, buttons are effective decorations. Selected with care for their colors, shapes, and materials, they can be used to accent the theme of a craft or add a whimsical touch. Round buttons, of course, make good eyes for a stuffed animal or doll, but don't be limited by convention. Treated as imaginative details, unusual buttons—tiny animals, flowers, thimbles, or fish, perhaps—will transform an ordinary sewing project into a work of art.

Yo-Yo Coverlet

Especially popular in the 1930s, yo-yo coverlets—which are pieced from hundreds of puffed fabric circles—offer a good way to take advantage of sewing-basket scraps. They are also easy to make, requiring little sewing experience. Each circle, or yo-yo, is simply basted along the edge, pulled into a puff, and then flattened with an iron. The arrangement of the yo-yos is usually random, as in the coverlet shown here. All the needlework can be done by hand, and no batting, backing, or quilting is necessary; when the yo-yos are joined, the coverlet is finished.

◆ IMPORTANT INFORMATION

The coverlet shown here measures 72 x 108 inches. To figure the coverlet size you would like to make, first measure the length and width of your mattress top. Next, figure the measurement for the side overhang. (This measurement is usually 13 inches to 15 inches for a standard mattress, but it depends on the style of the bed frame and whether or not you use a dust ruffle.) Double this measurement and add the number to the mattress width. Next, figure the measurement for the overhang at the foot of the bed and the amount you need to tuck under the pillows (be generous). Add these two measurements to the mattress length.

You can use scraps, or yardage that you have purchased specifically for the coverlet, but be sure to choose medium-weight, firmly woven cottons that are not overly crisp. If the fabric is too stiff, the edges of the yo-yos will not turn attractively, and if it is too soft, the yo-yos will not hold their shape. Preshrink your fabrics, and avoid mixing fabrics that have a markedly different drape or weight.

The yo-yo circles are traced from a template 4 inches in diameter; after the circles are cut, gathered, and flattened, they measure just under two inches in diameter. You will need 361 circles for each square yard, which will be arranged in 19 rows of 19 yo-yos. A yard of 45-inch-wide fabric should yield 99 four-inch circles. The fabrics can be layered so that you are able to cut several circles at once; you will need to test how many layers your scissors will cut through with ease. Alternating the steps—cutting, gathering, and joining just enough yo-yos to make a small portion of the coverlet at one time—will make the process more fun.

◆ MATERIALS AND EQUIPMENT

Assorted cotton fabric, 22 yards total,
  45 inches wide
Lightweight cardboard
Thread

Tracing paper
Scissors
Sewing needle

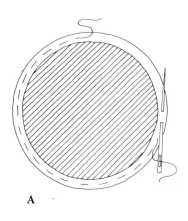

A

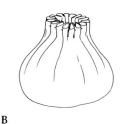

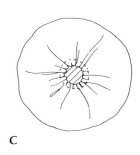

C

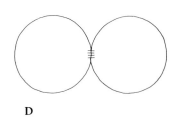

B

D

◆ DIRECTIONS

1. *Making the template:* Using a pencil, trace the Yo-Yo Pattern below onto the tracing paper and cut out. Place the paper pattern on the cardboard, draw around it, and cut out along the line.

2. *Cutting the fabric:* With the wrong sides up, stack the fabrics on a worktable. Place the template on the stack and draw around it, moving the template along until you have covered the surface with circles. Remove the template, pin the layers together, and cut out the circles along the line through all the layers.

3. *Making the yo-yos:* Press a generous ⅛ inch around the edge of a fabric circle to the wrong side. Using a double thread, baste all around through the folded edge (Illustration A). Pull the stitching, forming gathers, until the circle closes (right side out) and forms a puff (Illustration B). Knot the thread to secure the gathers. Flatten the puff into a yo-yo (Illustration C) and press to keep flat. Repeat to make more yo-yos.

4. *Joining the yo-yos:* With the gathered sides down, place two of the yo-yos side by side. Begin sewing by passing the needle through one yo-yo opening, to hide the knot, and bringing it up at the side of the yo-yo. Where the sides touch, sew the yo-yos together with three or four tiny overcast stitches (Illustration D). Continue joining the yo-yos in this manner to form a row that measures the desired width of the coverlet. Make several rows, then join the rows, matching the sides of the yo-yos in the same manner as above, until the coverlet is the desired length. ◆

YO-YO PATTERN

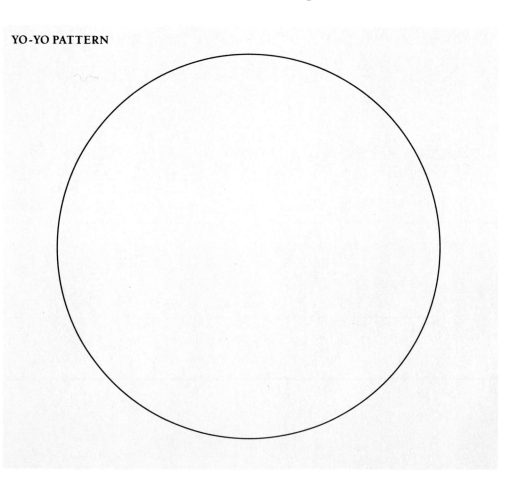

Log Cabin Doll Quilt

I n the 19th century, young girls who were learning to sew often tried their hand at a doll quilt because the small size made it less daunting to a novice seamstress than a full-size bed quilt. The doll quilt shown above is worked in the Log Cabin pattern, an American favorite named for the familiar log structures associated with pioneer days. Each quilt block is composed of fabric strips, or "logs," which are "built" around a central square; tradition holds that the square represents the chimney or hearth. Graduated in length, the strips in a Log Cabin pattern block are sewn on one at a time, with each end butting against the side of the previous strip so that the block grows outward in a kind of squared-off spiral.

One half of the strips in each block are traditionally light in color and the other half are dark; the light and dark areas divide the block diagonally into triangles. As the Log Cabin blocks are assembled to make the overall design, the light and dark triangular halves of the blocks can be juxtaposed in a number of ways to create different effects. Here, the blocks are arranged in the Straight Furrows pattern, a Log Cabin variation characterized by diagonal stripes.

Along with varied household hints, Lydia Maria Child, the author of the 1833 volume The Girl's Own Book, *offered sage advice to young folk. Little girls "often have a great many small bits of cloth, and large remnants of time," she wrote, "which they don't know what to do with; and I think it is better for them to make cradle quilts for their dolls, or their baby brothers, than to be standing around, wishing they had something to do."*

◆ IMPORTANT INFORMATION

This doll quilt is composed of four Log Cabin blocks. The blocks are pieced separately, then sewn together to create a larger square that is set off by a solid-color border. The quilt, backed with contrasting fabric and finished with bias binding, measures about 14 inches square. Like many traditional Log Cabin quilts, it has no batting and is not actually quilted.

Each Log Cabin block is made with strips of fabric in six dark and five light colors. The directions that follow explain how to arrange the strips for one block. When you are making your quilt, you can piece all four blocks in the same fabrics, or vary the colors slightly, as in the quilt shown here. Choose tightly woven cotton fabrics in a variety of prints and solids and preshrink them before cutting. To avoid mixing up the strips for the different blocks, cut the strips for one block at a time and keep them in separate plastic bags.

Before you begin, be sure to read all the directions. Note that the full-size Log Cabin Block Patterns on page 27 include a ¼-inch seam allowance on all sides. The numbers on the Piecing Diagram on page 25 indicate the order in which the pattern pieces are joined; the repeating letters indicate strips to be cut from the same fabric. Pin and stitch all the pieces with the right sides together. When piecing the blocks, backstitch the ends of each seam to make them stronger. Remove the pins after stitching each seam and press the seam allowance toward the darker fabric whenever possible so that it will not show through the finished quilt top.

◆ MATERIALS AND EQUIPMENT

Assorted cotton fabric remnants, 8 inches x 24 inches each (6 dark colors and 5 light colors)
1 piece cotton fabric, 16 x 16 inches (for backing)
½ yard cotton fabric, 45 inches wide (for border and bias binding)
Thread

Lightweight cardboard
Plastic food storage bags
Tracing paper
Scissors
Dressmaker's pins
Dressmaker's chalk
Ruler

◆ DIRECTIONS

1. *Making the patterns:* Using a pencil, trace the Log Cabin Block Patterns on page 27 onto the tracing paper and cut out. Place the paper patterns on the cardboard, draw around them, and cut out along the lines. Transfer all the numbers to the cardboard patterns.

2. *Cutting the fabric:* Separate the dark and light fabrics. Using the chalk or a pencil, label the dark fabrics A, C, E, G, I, and K, and label the light fabrics B, D, F, H, and J. Refer to the Piecing Diagram below to be sure you understand the way in which the light and dark colors go together: pieces 1A and 2B are the same size, pieces 2B and 3B are the same color, and so on. With the wrong side up, place each piece of fabric on a worktable. Place the appropriate cardboard pattern on top and draw around it to mark the cutting lines. From fabric A, cut and label piece 1A. From fabric B, cut and label pieces 2B and 3B. From fabric C, cut and label pieces 4C and 5C. Continuing to refer to the Piecing Diagram, cut and label all the pieces for one block and place them in a plastic bag. Repeat for the remaining three blocks.

3. *Sewing the quilt blocks:* To begin making the quilt block, stitch piece 1A (the dark center square) to piece 2B. Referring to the Piecing Diagram, continue to join the pieces in numerical order. Stitch piece 3B to pieces 1A and 2B so that a square is formed. Then stitch piece 4C in place as shown in the Piecing Diagram. Continue to join the pieces in numerical order, working outward and counterclockwise from the center piece until you have used all the pieces for the block. Repeat to make the remaining three quilt blocks. Press all the blocks carefully on both sides.

4. *Assembling the quilt top:* With the right sides up, lay the four blocks out on the worktable with the dark and light halves arranged according to the Assembly Diagram below. Stitch the two upper blocks together and press the seam to the left.

Piecing Diagram

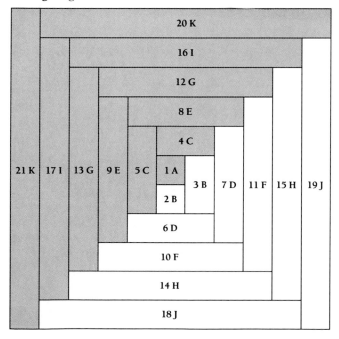

Assembly Diagram

Stitch the two lower blocks together and press the seam to the right. Referring to the Assembly Diagram, stitch the two 2-block units together, matching the center seams carefully. Press the seam to one side; press the four-block square carefully on both sides.

5. *Making the border:* Measure one side of the four-block square. From the border fabric, cut two strips, 1½ inches wide, to this measurement. Stitch the strips to the opposite sides of the four-block square and press the seams toward the border strips. Measure the remaining sides of the four-block square across the ends of the border strips you have already added. Cut two border strips, 1½ inches wide, to this measurement. Stitch the border strips to the remaining two sides of the four-block square and press the seams toward the border strips. Press the entire square carefully on both sides.

6. *Adding the backing:* With the wrong side up, lay the backing fabric on the worktable. With the right side up, center the four-block square on the backing, aligning the grain lines, and pin. Using the ruler and a pencil, mark a square on the backing fabric ¼ inch outside the four-block square. Cut out the backing along this line. Baste the four-block square to the backing along all sides. Remove the pins.

7. *Making the bias binding:* Trim the binding fabric into a rectangle with all four edges cut on the straight grain. Fold the rectangle diagonally so that the crosswise grain aligns with the lengthwise grain (Illustration A). Crease along the fold (bias) line, unfold the fabric, and mark the bias line with the pencil and ruler. Draw lines parallel to this bias line at 2-inch intervals to mark the bias strips; mark enough strips to total 64 inches in length and cut them out. To join two bias strips, place them at right angles to each other with the right sides together and stitch across the end with a ¼-inch seam allowance (Illustration B). Repeat until all the strips are joined. Press the seams open.

8. *Binding the quilt:* Square off one end of the bias binding strip and fold ¼ inch to the wrong side; press. With the right sides together, place the folded end of the bias strip at the center of one edge of the quilt top, aligning the raw edges of the binding and quilt backing. With a ½-inch seam allowance, stitch the binding to the quilt around all sides, allowing for mitered corners as you go. When you reach the point where you started, cut off any excess binding, leaving a small overlap.

9. *Finishing the binding:* Hold the quilt with the right side up and press the binding toward the edges, folding the pleats at the corners into neat miters. Fold the binding over the edge of the quilt, mitering the corners on the back. Fold under the raw edge of the binding ⅜ inch and pin to the backing. Slipstitch the folded edge against the stitching line and slipstitch the mitered corners. Remove the pins and press both sides of the quilt. ◆

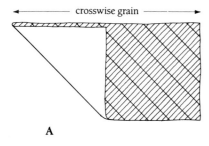

A

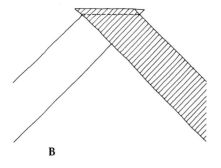

B

LOG CABIN BLOCK PATTERNS

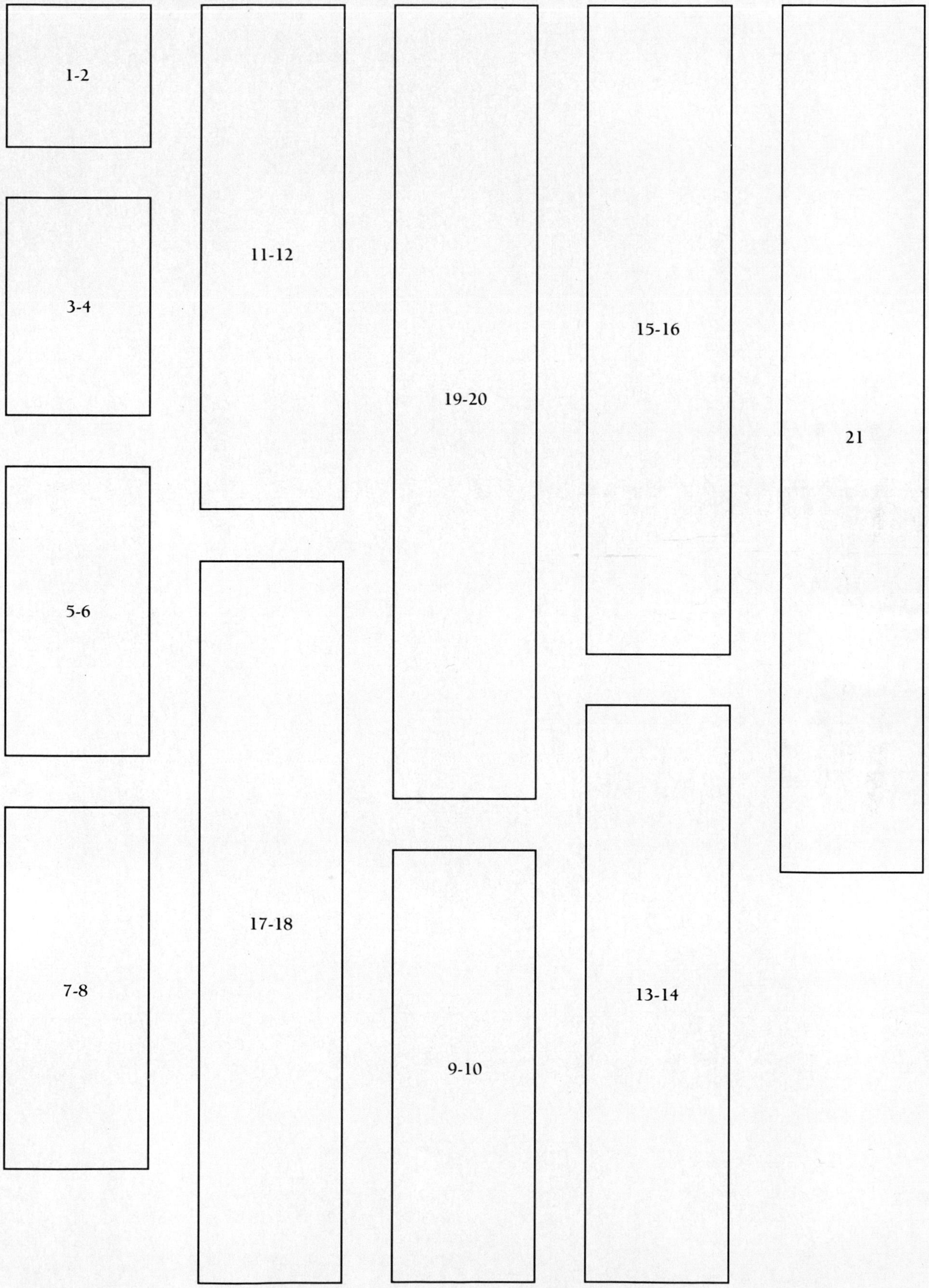

1-2

3-4

5-6

7-8

11-12

17-18

19-20

9-10

15-16

13-14

21

TEA-DYEING FABRIC

Tea-dyeing is a good way to give the mellowed appearance of age to the fabric and trimmings you plan to use for handcrafted folk toys and quilts. The light, warm tint produced by the tea helps tone down the bright colors in new fabrics and does the same for pure whites.

Dyeing with tea is very simple to do. The process works best on 100 percent cotton or linen; cotton blends can also be used, but they generally take longer to absorb color. Be sure to prewash your cloth to remove any sizing, and test-dye a small sample of fabric to see how the color takes before putting all of it in the tea.

The amount of tea you need will vary according to the amount of fabric you are dyeing. For half a yard of 45-inch-wide cotton, three to five tea bags steeped in a quart of water should suffice (use more tea bags if you want a deeper color).

To begin, put the tea bags in a stain-resistant bowl or pan and add boiling water. After ten to twenty minutes, remove the tea bags and swirl the water to mix. To help ensure an evenly dyed color, soak the fabric in clear water and wring it out thoroughly before adding it to the tea; it should be wet but not dripping. Immerse the fabric and leave it in the tea, stirring it from time to time, until the cloth appears slightly darker than the color you desire; the color will lighten when the cloth dries. Remove the fabric, rinse it in cool water, and dry. Press to set the color.

Crazy Cat

This jaunty stuffed cat is made from wool crazy patchwork, which you can easily piece and embroider yourself. Sewn from fabric scraps, crazy patchwork was particularly popular in the late 19th century. The name refers to the haphazard manner in which the scraps were put together. Because the piecing followed no rule, crazy patchwork was faster to make than a geometric pieced pattern.

Crazy patchwork could be very elaborate and was often distinguished by decorative stitching on the piecing seams. The patches themselves might also be embroidered with small bouquets, butterflies, or other decorative motifs; such fancy embroidery was intended to show off the skill of the maker. Most crazy patchwork was made into decorative throws that were used on a piano or sofa. Patchwork toys sewn from fragments of worn-out throws probably first appeared in this century.

Considered quite fashionable, crazy patchwork was generally made by well-to-do ladies with plenty of leisure time. The materials were usually elegant; bits of silk, satin, ribbon, and even lace found their way from scrap baskets (or purchased kits) into the finished work. Occasionally, crazy patchwork was pieced in wool or cotton, but woolen patchwork tended to be utilitarian rather than showy. Wool makes a good choice for a patchwork toy, however, because it holds up well.

◆ IMPORTANT INFORMATION

Choose wool fabric scraps that are similar in weight, and avoid coat fabrics. (You may use silks and satins if you wish to make a fancier cat.) The scraps should be at least 1½ inches and not more than 3½ inches in width for this project; this will ensure that each pattern piece will consist of at least two different fabrics and that the seams will not be so close together that the patchwork becomes bulky.

For this 11-inch-tall cat, you will need enough scraps to piece together a 20 x 40-inch rectangle. You can piece the rectangle first and then cut all the full-size cat patterns from it, or you can piece a number of smaller sections and cut the patterns a few at a time. The larger the piece of "crazy" fabric you make, the more flexibility you will have in planning the way the patches fall in the patterns. If you use smaller patchwork sections, each one should be large enough to accommodate the same pattern twice (each pattern is cut in reverse to make the left and right sides of the cat).

Once the fabric is pieced, it is fused to interfacing to stabilize the grain lines and keep the seams from splitting when the pattern pieces are cut out. After the pattern pieces are cut from the patchwork, the seams are embellished with embroidery. Here, buttons are used for the eyes, but if you are making the cat for a small child the eyes should be embroidered or painted on with acrylic paint.

Pin and stitch all the pieces, right sides together, with a ¼-inch seam allowance. Backstitch the beginning and end of each seam and press the seams open as you work.

In 1864, during the crazy quilt craze, the editors of Godey's Lady's Book reminded readers that their fancywork projects were "not Trifles but arts that, elevating human feeling above animal instincts, make men and women better and families happier."

◆ MATERIALS AND EQUIPMENT

Assorted fabric scraps

1½ yards fusible interfacing

One 12-ounce package polyester stuffing

1 yard ribbon, ¾ to 1 inch wide

2 buttons, about ½ inch in diameter

*1 skein 6-strand embroidery floss in
    desired color*

Thread

Tracing paper

Scissors

Embroidery needle

Sewing needle

Dressmaker's chalk

◆ DIRECTIONS

1. *Making the patterns:* Using a pencil, trace the Crazy Cat Patterns on pages 34-37 onto the tracing paper. Mark all the dots, letters, notches, and numbers. Cut out the paper patterns along the lines, cutting the notches outward.

2. *Making the crazy patchwork:* Begin the crazy piecing by trimming two fabric scraps so that they have straight edges where you wish to join them. The seams need not be on the straight grain, but bear in mind that bias edges tend to stretch, so plan to join a bias edge to an edge on the straight grain. With right sides together, stitch two pieces together. Decide where you wish to join the next piece, and trim an edge there. Continue joining pieces in this manner to make an interesting "crazy" pattern.

3. *Fusing the interfacing:* When you have pieced the crazy patchwork to the desired size, fuse the interfacing to the fabric following the manufacturer's directions.

4. *Cutting the fabric:* With the right side up, lay the pieced, fused fabric on a worktable. Place one paper pattern on the fabric, adjusting it until you like the way it falls on the piecing. Pin and cut around it, cutting the notches outward. Mark all dots and letters onto the wrong side of the cut piece. Remove the pins. Reverse the pattern and lay it on the right side of the fabric again. Pin, cut, and mark as above. Repeat for all the patterns, being sure to reverse the patterns as you go. (Copy the markings for the face onto only one of the two head pieces.)

5. *Embellishing the seams:* Using the embroidery needle and three strands of the embroidery floss, embellish the seams of the crazy patchwork in the body pieces with herringbone stitch. To work herringbone stitch (Illustration A), hold the fabric right side up and bring the needle up from the wrong side at point 1 about ⅛ inch to the right side of the seam. Make a ¾-inch stitch diagonally across the seam, inserting the needle at point 2. Bring the needle up at point 3 to make a small stitch. Make a ¾-inch stitch diagonally across the seam to point 4. Continue, spacing the stitches evenly so that the diagonals are parallel, until the seam is decorated. In this manner, decorate as many seams as you wish.

6. *Making the cat front:* On the left Upper Front/Paw (Pattern 1), reinforce the corner marked A with a short angled line of machine stitching and clip the corner to

Herringbone Stitch

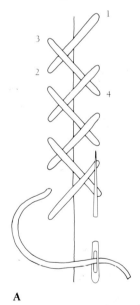

A

the dot. Stitch the left Upper Front/Paw to the left Paw Back (Pattern 2) between dots A and B, stitching around the paw and up to the neck edge. On the left Lower Front (Pattern 3), reinforce the corner marked A with a short angled line of machine stitching and clip the corner to the dot. Stitch the left Upper Front/Paw to the left Lower Front between dots A and C, then stitch the left Lower Front to the left Paw Back between dots A and D. Repeat to make the right front section of the cat. Stitch the left front section to the right front section along the center front seam between dots E and F.

7. *Making the cat back:* Stitch together the Back pieces (Pattern 4) along the center back seam between dots G and H.

8. *Joining the cat front and back:* Stitch the front and back together at the side seams from the neck edge at dot J around the back haunch to dot K, leaving the lower edge open between the K dots.

9. *Embroidering the cat face:* On one Head piece (Pattern 5), embroider the cat face using the embroidery needle and floss. Use four long stitches for the nose and six lines of stem stitching for the whiskers. To work stem stitch (Illustrations B-1 and B-2), hold the fabric right side up and bring the needle up from the wrong side at point 1. Making a ¼-inch stitch, insert the needle at point 2. Bring the needle up at point 3 halfway between points 1 and 2 and draw through, holding the floss to the left of the needle. Making a ¼-inch stitch, put the needle in at point 4. Bring the needle up again at point 2 in the hole made by the floss going in previously, and draw through, still holding the floss to the left of the needle. Continue in this manner until you have stitched whiskers about an inch long. Sew on the buttons for eyes.

10. *Making the cat head:* Stitch the head front to the head back, up from one dot L, around the ears, and to the other dot L. Clip the corners between the ears and turn the head right side out.

11. *Joining the head and the body:* With the right sides together (the body wrong side out), pin the head to the body, matching the center chin at the notch to the center front seam at dot E, and matching the center back nape at the notch to the center back seam at dot G, aligning the raw edges and easing the body to fit. Stitch and remove the pins.

12. *Making the tail:* Stitch together the Tail pieces (Pattern 6), leaving the straight end open between dots H and M. Turn the tail right side out, using the eraser end of the pencil to push the fabric through the opening. Using some of the polyester stuffing, pack the tail firmly, but leave the open end empty enough to flatten and stitch closed.

13. *Attaching the tail:* Place the tail in the center back seam, matching dots H and M so that the tail curves down. Stitch the center back seam closed through the tail to the end of the seam.

14. *Stuffing the cat:* Turn the cat body right side out. Using the stuffing, pack firmly, starting with the paws, then filling the ears, the head, and the body. Pin closed the opening at the bottom, checking to see that the cat sits well. Stitch closed by hand. Remove the pins. Tie the ribbon in a bow around the neck. ◆

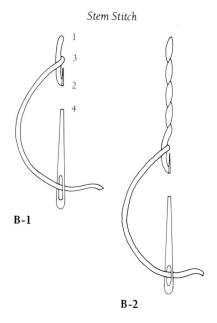

Stem Stitch

B-1

B-2

Topsy-Turvy Doll

Topsy-turvy dolls have delighted children since the 1800s. These unusual cloth toys are composed of two half dolls that are joined together at the waist (a reversible skirt flips to reveal one head and torso at a time). Much of the appeal of the dolls is found in the playful ways their makers chose to highlight the idea of "opposites," varying the types of figures depicted and choosing fabrics in contrasting colors or prints for the doll clothes. The doll to be made here is a contemporary adaptation of one of the most popular topsy-turvy combinations, a black girl and a white girl. (For more information on topsy-turvy dolls, see pages 42-43.)

◆ IMPORTANT INFORMATION

This topsy-turvy doll is about 11 inches tall from head to hem. You will need solid black cotton and natural-colored muslin for the bodies, two different calico prints for the reversible skirt, and striped cottons in contrasting colors for the waistbands. Both halves of the doll are made from the same full-size pattern. A simple skirt is gathered from a two-sided rectangle of cloth; a heart embroidered in red forms the bodice. Stitch all seams with a ¼-inch seam allowance.

◆ MATERIALS AND EQUIPMENT

2 pieces muslin fabric, 9 x 9 inches each
2 pieces black cotton fabric, 9 x 9 inches each
2 pieces calico fabric, 9 x 20½ inches each
  (for reversible skirt)
2 pieces striped cotton fabric, 1½ x 6¼ inches
  each in contrasting colors (for waistbands)
6-strand embroidery floss, 1 skein each
  in red, black, and rust
Thread
One 12-ounce package polyester stuffing

Acrylic paint in white and brown
6-inch embroidery hoop
Tracing paper
Dressmaker's carbon paper in white and
  blue
Scissors
Sewing needle
Embroidery needle
Fine-tipped paintbrush

◆ DIRECTIONS

1. *Making the pattern:* Using a pencil, trace the Topsy-Turvy Doll Pattern on page 41 onto the tracing paper; cut out. Mark the grain line, heart, eyes, and mouth.

2. *Marking the fabric:* With the wrong side up, place one of the two muslin pieces on a worktable. Place the paper pattern on the muslin, aligning the grain lines, and draw around it. Holding the pattern in place, slide the blue carbon face-up under

the muslin and transfer the heart, eyes, and mouth to the right side of the fabric by drawing over them with the pencil. Repeat for one of the black cotton fabric pieces, using the white carbon.

3. *Embroidering the hearts:* With the marked side up, place the muslin in the embroidery hoop, centering the heart. Using the embroidery needle and three strands of the red embroidery floss, bring the needle up from the wrong side at the heart point. Insert the needle at the center of the notch of the heart. Bring the needle up from the wrong side as close as possible to the left of the first stitch at the bottom of the heart and reinsert it as close as possible to the left of the first stitch at the top of the heart. Continue in this manner until the left half of the heart is filled, keeping the stitches straight and smooth. Embroider the right half of the heart in the same manner. Repeat to make the heart on the black cotton fabric piece.

4. *Cutting out the doll bodies:* With the right sides together, place the embroidered muslin piece on the unembroidered muslin piece and pin the two layers together inside the pattern outline. Cut out the doll body along the line, remove the pins, and separate the pieces. Repeat for the black cotton fabric pieces. With the right sides together, pin the embroidered muslin body front to the embroidered black body front at the waist edge only and stitch together. Repeat for the body backs. Remove the pins.

5. *Adding the hair:* With the right sides up, place the pair of doll backs on the worktable (Illustration A). Cut six 3-inch lengths of the black embroidery floss and lay three lengths at each temple of the black doll head, aligning the ends with the raw edge. Baste in place ¼ inch from the raw edge. Cut about thirty 3-inch lengths of the rust embroidery floss and lay them at even intervals around the white doll head, aligning the ends with the raw edge. Baste in place ¼ inch from the raw edge.

6. *Joining the doll bodies:* With the right sides together, lay the pair of doll fronts carefully over the pair of doll backs and pin. Stitch all the way around, leaving a 2-inch opening on one side of the waist for turning and stuffing. Remove the pins and trim the seams to ⅛ inch; clip the inner curves at ¼-inch intervals. Turn the bodies right side out. Pack tightly with the polyester stuffing, using the end of the paintbrush to poke the stuffing into the arms first. Slipstitch the opening in the side closed.

7. *Finishing the heads:* Braid the floss on the black head into two braids, and tie with bows of red floss. Trim the rust floss on the white head evenly, tie it into a ponytail, and add a bow of black floss. Using the brush and brown paint, mark the eyes and mouth on the white face. Using the white paint, repeat for the black face.

8. *Making the skirt:* Baste two rows along one long edge of one calico fabric piece ¼ inch and ⅛ inch in from the raw edge. Repeat for the other calico piece. With the right sides together, lay one calico piece over the other, aligning the basted edges. Stitch on the edge opposite the basting. Press the pieces open. With the right sides together, refold perpendicular to the seam. Stitch along the long edges opposite the fold 2 inches in from each end to make a tube (Illustration B). Press this seam open. Turn the tube right side out.

9. *Making the waistbands:* Fold under ¼ inch on one end of one waistband strip and press. Press under ¼ inch on the long sides. Bring the long sides together, folded edges in, and press again. Repeat for the other waistband.

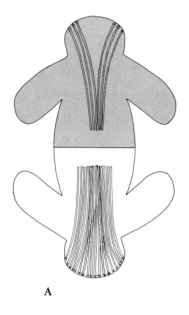

A

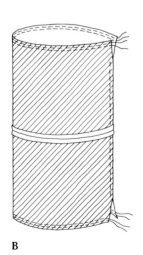

B

10. *Attaching the waistbands:* On one basted skirt edge, pull the stitching to form gathers until the edge measures 6 inches. Insert one raw edge into one folded waistband, pin, and topstitch through all the layers along the bottom edge of the waistband (Illustration C). Repeat for the other basted skirt edge. Remove the pins. Invert the tube halfway, wrong sides together, to align both waistbands. Press, and topstitch along the bottom edge of the skirt.

11. *Attaching the skirt:* Place the skirt on the doll, tightening each waistband under the arms by overlapping the ends and slipstitching each waistband closed. ◆

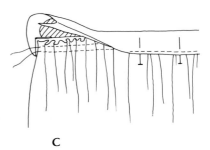

C

TOPSY-TURVY DOLL PATTERN

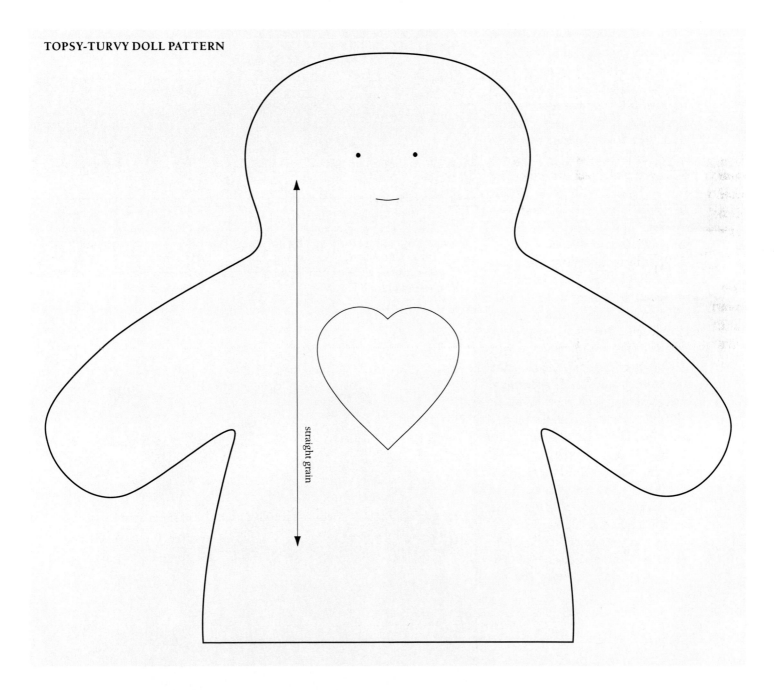

straight grain

TOPSY-TURVY VARIATIONS

Like many folk toys, topsy-turvy dolls are obscure in origin. It is thought that these two-headed dolls with reversible skirts first became popular just after the Civil War. The unusual form may have derived from 18th-century Pennsylvania hex dolls, which had two heads (usually one animal and one human) and were used for casting spells. Because topsy-turvy dolls typically combine black and white figures, the name is frequently associated with Topsy, the slave child in Harriet Beecher Stowe's 1852 novel, *Uncle Tom's Cabin*. However, the term had been used to mean upside down long before the book was ever written.

While many examples were homemade, topsy-turvys were also mass-produced, beginning in 1899. Marketed under such names as Dolly Double and Tu-N-One, they were available at major toy stores as well as through mail-order companies like Montgomery Ward. There were many variations on the black-and-white combination: one version featured Red Riding Hood, whose skirt doubled back to reveal the hungry wolf; another combined the Goddess of Liberty with Uncle Sam. Some dolls could be purchased as kits that included lithographed cotton body pieces and prestamped dress fabric ready to be cut and assembled. (To make your own topsy-turvy doll, see page 39.)

Seen "topsy" above and "turvy" below, this black-white doll was manufactured around 1900. The fabric faces were printed and molded and then stitched on like masks to imitate more expensive china dolls.

Although the two characters in the c. 1900 topsy-turvy doll above and below wear different outfits, their full skirts and aprons are made of matching fabric. The hats and aprons are removable; the dresses are not.

The homemade topsy-turvy doll above and below is a well-loved toy. What the doll lacks in elegance it makes up for in character. Interestingly, the doll's two dresses are sewn from different versions of the same printed fabric.

This doll was probably made from a kit. The chromolithographed faces depict a happy baby, above, and a crying baby, below. The glad-sad combination is one of the several variations popularized by manufacturers.

Relatively new, this homemade doll combines Goldilocks, above, with the Three Bears, below. Storybook characters have long been favorite subjects for both manufactured and hand-crafted topsy-turvy dolls.

Embroidery

traditional canvas work and counted-thread stitchery

Although embroidery, the embellishment of a textile with ornamental stitches, requires practice and patience, most of the techniques are not difficult to learn. Depending on your level of skill and creativity, the stitches you make can be simple or complex, and the designs that result, monochromatic or richly hued.

This chapter offers the opportunity to try four embroidery projects. Three of the pieces—the traditional cross-stitch sampler, the easy Irish-stitch footstool cover, and the more complicated needlepoint bellpull—are worked in different forms of counted-thread stitchery, in which you follow a chart to stitch a design onto unmarked fabric. The fourth project, an outline-work hand towel, involves tracing a design onto a cloth and then embroidering it.

If you are new to embroidery, plan to practice the stitches until you feel comfortable with them. You will find that once such handwork is mastered, it can be a satisfying pastime.

Irish stitch, or bargello, makes an attractive covering for a footstool (see pages 64-67). The cardboard horseshoe at center is a needlecase.

Cross-Stitch Sampler

In the 18th and early 19th centuries, a mastery of needlework was considered an important part of a young lady's education. At an early age, she was taught to stitch letters and numerals into a sampler; when older, she would use this skill for marking her household linens. Some samplers served as a kind of personal pattern reference, while others were used as practice pieces on which the needleworker might work to perfect a particular stitch or to experiment with a new motif. The more elaborate samplers included verses and intricate pictorial scenes.

The sampler shown here is worked entirely in cross-stitch, among the simplest of the many stitches that might be incorporated into a sampler. The design has been adapted from a sampler made around 1820 by a Pennsylvania girl named Ruth Hide, who was probably about twelve years old when she worked it. The strawberry vine border and alphabets are typical of motifs found on many American samplers of the period.

Not every little girl who embroidered a sampler enjoyed the task. Around 1800, ten-year-old Patty Polk, of Kent County, Maryland, stitched a piece with the words, "Patty Polk did this and she hated every stitch she did in it. She loves to read much more."

◆ IMPORTANT INFORMATION

Cross-stitch is a type of counted-thread embroidery in which the needleworker follows a chart, placing the stitches by counting threads in the background fabric; the design is not transferred to the fabric before it is stitched. The embroidery is worked on an even-weave fabric, which has the same number of threads running lengthwise and crosswise in each square inch. Any even-weave fabric in a count of from six to over thirty threads per inch can be used. The count of the fabric determines the number of stitches in one inch—the lower the count, the larger the stitch—which in turn determines the size of the finished embroidered design.

This sampler is worked on 25-count linen. Each stitch is made over the intersection of two lengthwise and two crosswise threads, and the design area measures $9\frac{1}{2}$ x $13\frac{1}{2}$ inches. (If you were to stitch over a single-thread intersection, the design area would measure half that size.) To make the sampler, you will need to follow the Design Chart on pages 54-55. Each square in the grid represents one cross-stitch. The different symbols in the squares represent the different colors in the Color Key on page 55.

When working cross-stitch, you will find it easier to keep an even stitch tension with the linen firmly secured in an embroidery hoop. To prevent permanent creases from forming in the linen, remove the embroidery from the hoop when you are not actually cross-stitching. Separate the embroidery floss into two-strand pieces—use 18-inch lengths—and work with two strands throughout. Never knot the floss; instead, leave a 1-inch tail at the back that will be secured as you stitch. To secure the other end of the floss when you are finished, slide the needle under several stitches on the back of the work and trim the floss. If you do not know how to do cross-stitch, refer to the section Learning to Cross-Stitch on page 52 and practice on a scrap of linen.

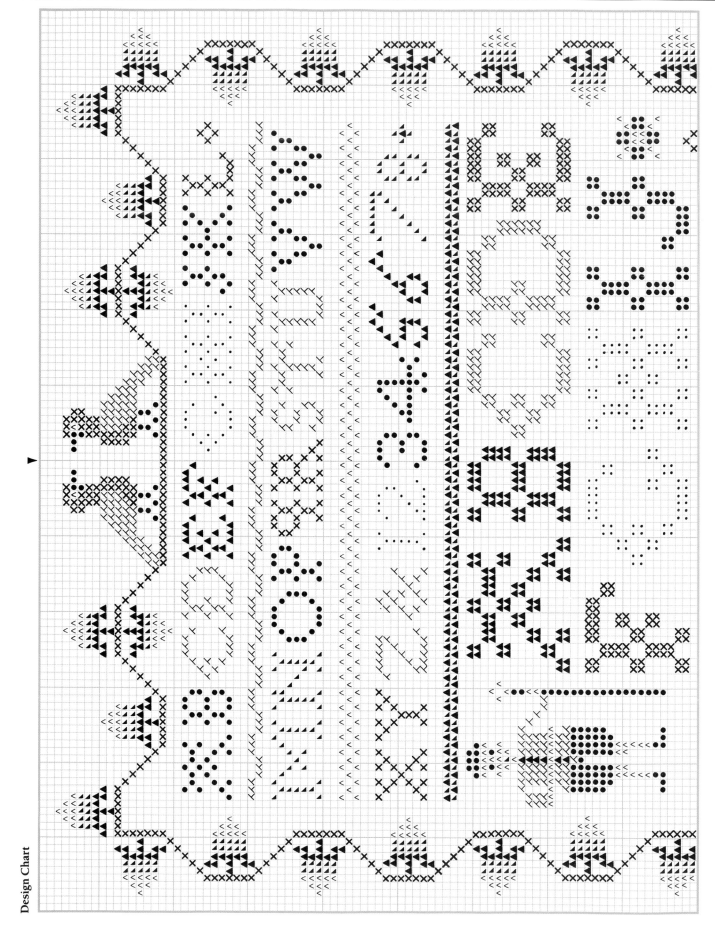

Design Chart

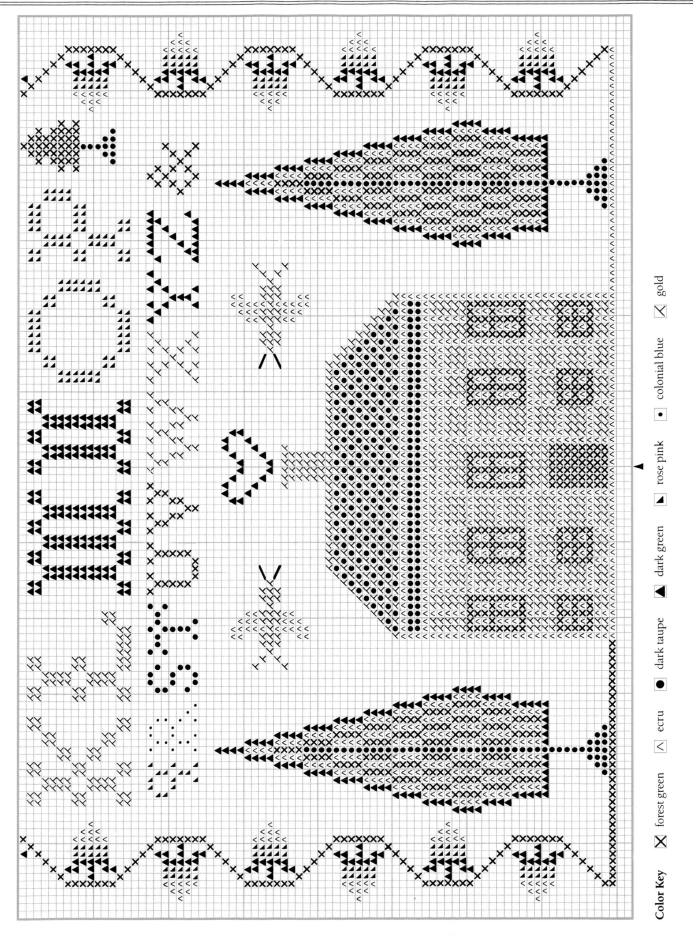

Color Key

✗ forest green	∧ ecru	● dark taupe	▲ rose pink	⊠ gold
	✕ dark green	▲ dark green	• colonial blue	

STITCHES
IN TIME

Although the tradition of stitching embroidered samplers was introduced to the colonies in the 1600s by English and European settlers, many distinctively American styles of samplers developed. Genealogical samplers like those shown here, for example, are believed to have originated in this country, first appearing in the 1770s. It was not until the mid-19th century that similar types were made in England.

Sometimes called family registers or family records, genealogical samplers were particularly popular between about 1800 and 1830. Intended to be displayed on a wall as decoration, they are typically distinguished by ambitious designs of flowers or landscapes, and those conceived as memorials often feature willows and neoclassical columns and urns. (Following the death of George Washington in 1799, expressions of mourning became fashionable.)

For the most part, genealogical samplers were the products of pri-

The floral vine on Elizabeth Dana's "family register" above was a popular style of border for New England samplers. Lorenza Fisk's family-tree sampler at right displays golden apples; it is one of twenty similar works known to have been made in the Lexington-Concord area of Massachusetts.

vate academies in New England and in Pennsylvania, where schoolgirls studied needle arts, reading, and music. A teacher might draw the designs on linen for her students to stitch in silk or linen thread, or the girls themselves would copy borders and pictures from engravings or from existing needlework pieces. Because the samplers made in a particular academy were often very similar to one another, it is sometimes possible to trace a sampler's origin even if the name of the school or town does not appear on the work. The stitched words—arranged in neat columns, placed in tidy boxes, or worked on apples growing from the "family tree"—generally record a couple's wedding date and the names and birth dates of their children. Some samplers also contain plaintive references to childhood deaths or verses that read as pious reminders of the passing of time. "Perhaps what goodness gives to-day," warns one, "Tomorrow goodness takes away."

Azubah G. Capen was about sixteen when she made the "family record" above at Miss Glover's school in Stoughton, Massachusetts. Elizabeth Newman's sampler at left combines genealogical information with the weeping willows and funerary urns that appeared in 19th-century mourning pictures.

Decorated Hand Towels

The hand towels shown here are embellished with outline work, a style of embroidery that resembles line drawing. Outline work can be sewn in a variety of stitches, but is always done in one color—usually red. Easy and quick, it became popular in America around 1880, and was favored for decorating bed and table linens.

Outline work was considered a particularly artistic form of embroidery because the designs, which were worked from printed patterns, relied upon well-drawn images. Pictures by Kate Greenaway, a well-known 19th-century British book illustrator, were frequently reproduced as patterns for outline work. Other designs were inspired by the type of linens they embellished: the words "good night" and "good morning" might be worked on a pillowcase, or pictures of chinaware stitched onto place mats.

◆ IMPORTANT INFORMATION

These fringed towels measure 18 x 36 inches and are made from white linen, although any firmly woven, lightweight (but not sheer) fabric can be used. To stitch the floral border, you will need to trace the full-size Border Pattern on pages 60-61 onto the fabric. Use a fabric-marking pen with nonpermanent ink that disappears when dampened (such pens are available in the notions department of most variety stores). Test the pen on a scrap of your fabric before tracing the pattern onto the towel.

Three stitches are used for the border: chain stitch for the round buds, stem stitch for the stem, leaf, and petal outlines, and French knots for the dots. You will find it easier to keep an even stitch tension with the linen firmly secured in an embroidery hoop. To prevent permanent creases from forming in the linen, remove the embroidery from the hoop when you are not stitching. Separate the embroidery floss into three-strand pieces—use 18-inch lengths—and stitch with three strands throughout. Never knot the floss; instead, leave a 1-inch tail at the back that will be secured as you stitch. To secure the other end of the floss when you are finished, slide the needle under several stitches on the back of the work and trim the thread. If you do not know how to do the three stitches, refer to the section Learning the Stitches on page 60 and practice on a scrap of fabric before beginning a towel.

◆ MATERIALS AND EQUIPMENT

1 piece lightweight white linen, 22 x 36 inches
2 skeins red 6-strand embroidery floss
6-inch embroidery hoop
Thread
Scissors

Embroidery needle
Tracing paper
Nonpermanent-ink fabric-marking pen
Black fine-point marking pen
Dressmaker's pins

Chain Stitch

A

Stem Stitch

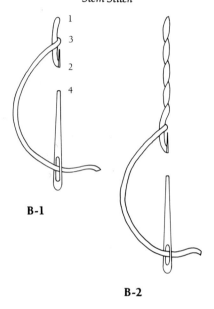

B-1

B-2

◆LEARNING THE STITCHES

1. *Getting started:* Secure a scrap of linen in the embroidery hoop.

2. *Working chain stitch:* Referring to Illustration A, bring the needle up from the back of the linen at point 1. Form a loop with the floss and insert the needle again at point 1, holding the loop against the linen with a finger; in the same motion, bring the needle up ¹⁄₁₆ inch away at point 2, and draw the floss through, catching the loop on the surface. Continue in this manner, always inserting the needle back into the hole just made, to make a chain of "links." Anchor the last link with a small stitch.

3. *Working stem stitch:* Referring to Illustration B-1, bring the needle up from the back of the linen at point 1. Making a ¹⁄₈-inch stitch, insert the needle at point 2. Bring the needle up at point 3 halfway between points 1 and 2, and draw the floss through, holding it to the left of the needle. Making a ¹⁄₈-inch stitch, insert the needle at point 4 and bring it up again at point 2 in the hole made by the previous stitch. Draw the floss through, still holding it to the left of the needle. Continue to work in this manner (Illustration B-2).

4. *Working French knots:* Referring to Illustration C-1, bring the needle up from the back of the linen at point 1. Holding the needle parallel to the linen and just above the fabric, wrap the floss around it once. Holding the floss so that it fits closely around the point of the needle, insert the needle back into the linen again at point 1 (Illustration C-2). Pull the needle through to the wrong side to finish the knot (Illustration C-3). Bring the needle up again where you wish to make another French knot, and repeat.

BORDER PATTERN

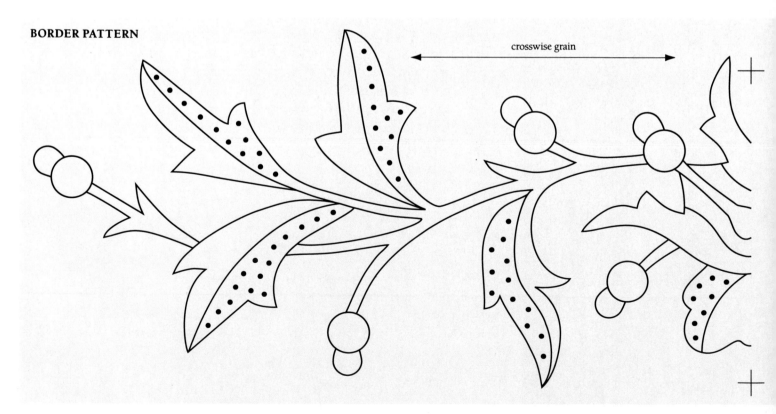

crosswise grain

French Knot

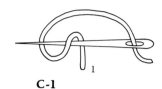

C-1

◆ TOWEL DIRECTIONS

1. *Preparing the linen:* To prevent the edges of the linen from raveling, secure them with zigzag or overcast stitching.

2. *Making the register marks:* Fold the linen in half lengthwise. Measure 3 inches in from one end and make a mark with the nonpermanent-ink pen on the fold, then measure in another 3¼ inches and make a second mark on the fold.

3. *Making the pattern:* Using a pencil, trace the Border Pattern below onto the tracing paper, aligning the two halves of the design in the middle according to the register marks. Also trace the register marks and the grain line. With the fine-point marking pen, go over the pencil lines to darken them so that you will be able to see them when the linen is placed over the pattern.

4. *Marking the linen:* Place the pattern on a worktable. Unfold the linen and place it over the pattern with the crosswise grain aligned, matching the register marks on the linen with those on the pattern. Pin. Using the nonpermanent-ink pen, trace the design onto the linen. Remove the pins.

5. *Embroidering the border:* Place the linen in the embroidery hoop, centering one end of the marked border design. Starting at this end, stitch over the marked lines, embroidering the entire design in a logical order. Work the round buds in chain stitch, the stem, leaf, and petal outlines in stem stitch (plan your stitches to meet neatly at the points of the leaves), and the dots in French knots. It is not necessary to cut the floss when changing stitches, but you should avoid carrying the floss from one design area to another on the back of the work.

6. *Hemming the long edges:* When all the embroidery is finished, press the

C-2

C-3

towel. With the design centered, trim the towel to be 18 inches wide. On each 36-inch edge, press ½ inch to the wrong side and stitch close to the fold with a small zigzag stitch. Trim the raw edge close to the stitching.

7. *Removing the ink markings:* Following the pen manufacturer's instructions, remove the ink markings. Press the towel again.

8. *Squaring the ends and making the fringe:* Trim the zigzag or overcast stitching from both ends of the towel. To square the towel, loosen the first thread along one cut edge and pull it free. If the thread you have pulled away did not run all the way across the end, keep pulling threads away until one does. The remaining crosswise threads will now be square with the sides of the towel. Trim the towel along the outermost thread, then pull away threads until you have made a ¾-inch-long fringe. Repeat at the other end of the towel.

9. *Securing the fringe with buttonhole stitch:* Referring to Illustration D, hold the towel with the right side up. At the right-hand edge of one fringed end, make a tiny stitch on the wrong side of the towel to secure the floss. Bring the needle up at point 1, passing it through the fringe but not the linen. Insert the needle into the linen ¼ inch from the woven edge, at point 2. Bring the needle up through the fringe again at point 1. Insert the needle into the linen ¼ inch from the woven edge at point 3, holding the floss in a loop against the fringe. Bring the needle through the fringe directly above point 3 at point 4, passing it through the loop of floss under the needle. Pull the floss through, forming a bar of floss along the woven edge. Continue in this manner, working across the end of the towel. When you run out of floss, knot it neatly on the wrong side, then begin a new strand, passing the needle through the fringe and under the bar of the previous stitch. Repeat at the opposite end of the towel.

10. *Finishing the towel:* When you have finished the buttonhole stitching, wash the towel in mild soapy water, rinse, and hang it to dry. When it is nearly dry, place the towel face down and press, spray-starching if desired. ◆

Buttonhole Stitch

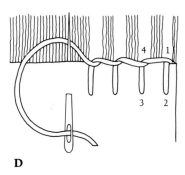

D

AN EMBROIDERED PAST

Embroidered hand towels, or *Handdicher,* like the three 19th-century pieces above, are a distinctive Pennsylvania-German folk art. Such handsome decorated linens were particularly popular from about 1820 to 1850. The long, narrow towels, which might be made from one to as many as six pieces of linen, were embroidered by adolescent girls, then set aside for their dowries. No two pieces are quite alike: the girls created their own designs, working them in counted cross-stitch, outline and herringbone stitches, and drawn work. The towels were often signed and dated, and a husband's name or initials might be added at the time of marriage. Most girls stitched only one towel.

Such *Handdicher* were intended for decoration rather than use, and loops or tabs were attached at the top so that the handiwork could be prominently displayed—traditionally on a door between the sitting room and the kitchen.

Irish-Stitch Footstool

Particularly popular in the 18th century in both Europe and America, Irish stitch was a favored form of embroidery for decorating upholstered furnishings. Now known variously as bargello, Hungarian stitch, flame stitch, or Florentine embroidery (all 20th-century terms), Irish stitch is characterized by straight, vertical stitches worked in multicolor zigzag patterns. The patterns vary widely; the footstool cover shown here is worked in a simple, randomly colored zigzag repeat.

◆ IMPORTANT INFORMATION

Irish stitch is a type of counted-thread embroidery in which the needleworker follows a chart, placing the stitches by counting threads in the background fabric; the design is not transferred to the fabric before it is stitched. The embroidery is worked on an even-weave fabric, which has the same number of threads running lengthwise and crosswise in each square inch. For Irish stitch, this fabric is most commonly an open canvas. The mesh count, or the number of threads per inch, determines the size of the stitch and the weight of the yarn to be used. The embroidery for this footstool is worked on 13-mesh bargello canvas. It is stitched with Persian wool, which is usually sold in 5-yard skeins. One skein will cover approximately 4 square inches of 13-mesh bargello canvas. To estimate the number of skeins you need, determine the number of square inches on your canvas and divide by four.

Many needlework shops sell footstools that are ready to be covered. You will need to cut your canvas to the size of the stool (see Step 1 in the Footstool Directions on page 66). To work the cover in the zigzag Irish-stitch pattern, you will need to follow the Design Chart on page 67, which represents a 33-stitch repeat. Each blue line in the grid represents one thread on the canvas; each vertical stitch is made over four horizontal threads of the canvas. The cover for the footstool shown measures 10 x 15 inches, but the 33 stitches can be repeated to cover a canvas of any dimension. It does not matter how the pattern breaks at the edge of the footstool, nor does it matter where or when you change colors. You can use as many colors as you like; change them often.

Separate the wool into two-ply pieces—use 18-inch lengths—and work with two plies throughout. Never knot the wool; instead, leave a 1-inch tail at the back that will be secured as you stitch. To secure the other end of the wool when you are finished, slide the needle under several stitches on the back of the work and trim. You may find it easier to control the stitch tension if you place the canvas in a frame. The stitches should lie evenly on the canvas; they should not be so loose that they will snag, or so tight that the canvas puckers. If you do not know how to do Irish-stitch embroidery, refer to the section Learning Irish Stitch on page 66 and practice on a scrap of canvas.

In 1755, Elizabeth Hinche advertised in the Boston Weekly News-Letter *that she "doth teach plain Sewing, Irish Stitch, Tent Stitch, Sampler Work, Embroidery, and other Sorts of Needle Work, if any Person sees fit to send their Children from the Country...."*

Needlepoint Bellpull

The 19th-century bellpull opposite is stitched in Berlin work, a type of needlepoint made from printed patterns, which originated in Germany in the early 1800s. The craze for Berlin work developed concurrently with the introduction of zephyr wools—soft, smooth, easy-to-dye tapestry wools spun from the fleece of merino sheep. Although both the patterns and the wools were manufactured in Germany, the popularity of Berlin work was international.

Berlin-work patterns were available for embroidering all manner of household furnishings, including rugs, upholstery, cushions, and bellpulls. In the Victorian era, bellpulls were a symbol of social standing; they not only allowed family members to ring for their servants, but also indicated to guests that servants were employed. Today, a needlepoint bellpull makes a handsome wall decoration.

◆ IMPORTANT INFORMATION

Needlepoint is a type of counted-thread embroidery in which the needleworker follows a chart, placing the stitches by counting threads in the background fabric; the design is not transferred to the fabric before it is stitched. The embroidery is worked on an even-weave fabric, which has the same number of threads running lengthwise and crosswise in each square inch. In needlepoint, this fabric is most commonly an open canvas. The mesh count, or the number of threads per inch, determines the size of the stitch and the weight of the yarn to be used. The embroidery for this bellpull is stitched with tapestry wool on 10-mesh needlepoint canvas.

To copy the bellpull opposite, you will need to refer to the Design Chart on pages 72-73. The bellpull measures 6¾ x 59 inches; the 14¾-inch floral design represented by the chart is done four times, worked from bottom to top. Each square in the grid represents one stitch; each stitch is made over a single-thread intersection on the canvas. The symbols represent the colors in the Color Key on page 73; the blank squares represent the taupe background.

This bellpull is embroidered with two basic needlepoint stitches. Basketweave (also called diagonal) stitch is used to fill in the background. This stitch creates a woven pattern on the wrong side of the work, which helps to stabilize the canvas, and is recommended for larger areas. Continental stitch is used for the symboled design. This stitch is not woven on the wrong side and is easier to work in smaller areas than basketweave stitch. The two stitches look identical on the right side of the work.

Never knot the wool; instead, leave a 1-inch tail at the back that will be secured as you stitch. To secure the other end of the wool, slide the needle under several stitches on the back and trim. The stitches should lie evenly; they should not be so tight that the canvas puckers, or so loose that the canvas threads show. If you do not know how to do needlepoint, refer to the section Learning Needlepoint on page 70 and practice on a scrap of canvas. Bellpull hangers are available at needlework shops.

74

Rugmaking

*time-honored methods
for crafting colorful carpets*

Braiding, hooking, and appliqué are rugmaking techniques that were commonly used during the 19th century. At that time, textiles were among the most valuable household possessions, and woolen scraps and worn clothing were saved and used to make rugs that were placed on tables as well as on floors.

Provided in this chapter are directions for all three techniques. To make a traditional braided rug, you cut and sew fabric strips, braid them, and then lace the braids together. For a hooked rug, you mark a design on a fabric foundation and then fill it in by pulling narrow loops of fabric through the foundation with a simple hook. And to craft a penny rug, you layer multicolored circles and stitch them to a backing. All of these rugmaking methods are easy enough for a beginner to master—even a child can help—and each yields a different effect, producing a rug with a distinctive look of its own.

*Bright wool circles, layered and stitched to a woolen backing, will yield
a handsome new penny rug (see pages 90-93).*

Braided Wool Rug

Although braided straw and cornhusk mats are mentioned in colonial records, there is very little documentation of braided fabric rugs before the 19th century, when they appeared on display at agricultural fairs. In 1826, Miss Lydia Hunt of Cranston, Rhode Island, was awarded a two-dollar prize at the state's Agricultural Society Fair for her innovative rag carpet. The admiring judges recorded that it "was manufactured from bits and odds and ends of every thing that would otherwise have been wholly useless, braided together, and its substantial fabric as well as economy was deemed worthy a premium." Apparently, many thrifty women used scraps for braiding rugs, but as factory-made fabrics became more readily available toward the middle of the century, rugmakers also began to purchase yard goods for braiding.

Braided rugs can be made in a variety of shapes. The most common—and easiest to braid—are circles and ovals. The directions that follow explain how to make an oval wool rug like the one in the center of the photograph at right; they can be adapted for an oval rug of any size.

◆ IMPORTANT INFORMATION

For ease in handling, a braided rug is assembled in interrelated steps. First, the fabric is cut into strips; the strips are then folded and braided, and the braids are laced together in stages. Before you begin, be sure to read all the directions so that you understand how the work progresses. While the steps may seem complicated, once you get started you will find the process quite simple.

In an oval rug, the length of the center braid determines the shape of the finished oval; the longer the center braid, the more elongated the oval shape will be. To determine the length of the center braid, first decide on the proportions of the rug you would like to make. Subtract the width from the length; to this measurement add 1 inch for each foot of width. The exact proportions of your finished rug may vary, depending on the weight of the fabric you are braiding.

When you are selecting the fabric for your rug, choose medium-weight, tightly woven woolens in harmonious colors. To determine the fabric yardage you will need, use this loose rule of thumb: 1 yard of medium-weight 54-inch-wide wool will equal about 1 square foot when braided. The rug featured here measures 4½ feet at its longest and 2½ feet at its widest, or approximately 11 square feet, and requires about 11 yards of 54-inch-wide wool to make. The weight of the fabric will dictate how wide you need to cut the strips, and thus the thickness of the braid. In general, the heavier the fabric, the wider the strip will need to be. (A strip width of between 2 and 3 inches is common.) You will need to make a sample braid to determine the correct strip width for your fabric. Do not use strips cut from fabrics of different weights because they will form uneven braids that are difficult to handle.

excess thread to finish. Rethread the same needle, bury the new knot inside the nearest cable, then switch the thread back to the lacing needle to continue.

6. *Joining the braid around the stub end:* Switch the thread back to the darning needle (since the stub end is a fold, not a cable, you cannot lace through it, but must sew the outer braid around it). Wrap the braid around the stub end smoothly, noting the extra cables that will have to be eased in. Stitch through one cable on the stub, then through one on the outer braid, then stitch again through the same two cables. Repeat so that each cable on the stub is attached to the second braid with two stitches, skipping cables on the outer braid as necessary to keep the turn smooth.

7. *Continuing the braid:* Turn the braided work right side up and continue braiding until the braid is long enough to wrap around the other end. Join additional wheels of strips to the working strips as necessary (be sure to sew the seams on the bias, as in Step 2). Switch the thread to the lacing needle and lace the braids together as in Step 5, stopping 4 inches short of the braided corner. Never make the braids more than 3 yards long before lacing them together or they will be too unwieldy to handle.

8. *Easing the braid around the curved ends:* Wrap the braid around the braided corner, noting the extra cables that will have be eased in. Ease in four cables at regular intervals, two on each side of the braided corner, by passing the lacing needle under two consecutive cables on the outer braid. Mark the eased cables with safety pins. Continue to braid and lace the rug until the braid is long enough to wrap around the next turn. Lace as in Step 7. Ease around the turn as above and continue braiding. When you are ready to ease around the next turn, space the extra cables so that they are not adjacent to those marked with the pins in the previous round and ease in six cables at regular intervals. Continue braiding, and ease around the next turn in the same manner, marking the eased cables with safety pins. Continue to braid and ease in the same manner, easing five cables at each end in the next round, and easing three cables at each end in the round after that. Continue to braid and lace, repeating the easing pattern of six, five, and three cables; reposition the safety pins as necessary. As the curves grow larger and shallower, the eased cables will be spaced farther and farther apart. This pattern will produce a flat, even rug with edges that will not ripple or roll up.

9. *Finishing the rug:* Continue braiding and lacing as in Step 8 until the rug is the desired size. Lace around one end of the rug and stop where the curve meets the side. Cut the strips from the wheels about 8 inches beyond this point. Remove the braid folders if you are using them. Unfold the strip ends, and cut them so that they gradually taper to nothing. Fold in the raw edges of the tapered strips, and using the sewing thread and sewing needle, stitch the folds in place. Braid the tapered strips, leaving the last 2 inches free, and lace to the rug, easing as necessary. Using the crochet hook, pull the loose ends into the cables on the wrong side and slipstitch with a few stitches to secure. ◆

OVERDYEING FABRICS

Above, wool strips have been overdyed in graduated shades of four different colors. The palest strips in each color group show the fabric before it was dyed.

To achieve the subtle shadings that give rug designs extra interest, rugmakers often recolor their fabrics by a process known as overdyeing. A particularly effective method of overdyeing is called shading. In shading, the fabric is cut into pieces and dyed in different strengths of the same color to produce varied but related tones. Braided together or hooked into the same area of a rug—traditionally the background—the shaded fabrics create an illusion of dimension that cannot be achieved with fabrics in a single color.

For the best results, overdyeing should be used only on pure wool fabrics. Choose a light-colored fabric and a dye color that is related to the fabric color. Any commercial fabric dye is appropriate, and one package is more than enough for overdyeing one yard of fabric. When dyeing, it is wise to wear rubber gloves and to cover the surfaces of your working area with newspaper. You will also need an enameled pot, a wooden spoon for stirring, and metal tongs for lifting the strips out of the dye.

To begin, prepare the dye in the pot full strength according to the manufacturer's directions. Cut your fabrics into pieces that are a manageable size—four or five inches wide—and cut a scrap for testing the strength of the dye. If you want an even color, you should wet the wool before dyeing it. Test the color, re-membering that the fabric will dry slightly lighter. Dilute the dye with boiling water if needed until you are satisfied with the strength—this will make your darkest color. Add some pieces of fabric. When the pieces are slightly darker than the color you desire, remove them from the dye, rinse them in cool water, and hang them to dry on a clothesline or rack. Dilute the dye to the next shade you want, then add more pieces. In this manner, continue diluting and dyeing until you have pieces in several graduated shades. Don't be overly concerned with achieving perfect results; the varied tones that can occur in dyeing will simply add character to your finished rug.

81

Black Cats Hooked Rug

Indigenous to North America, rug hooking is believed to have developed in the area of Maine and eastern Canada in the first half of the 19th century. Hooked rugs, made by pulling strips of fabric through a loosely woven backing, probably originated as inexpensive substitutes for the imported carpets that were fashionable at the time. The introduction of burlap bags, used by transatlantic shipping companies for transporting goods during this period, provided an ample supply of backing material for the rugmakers. Rug hooking eventually spread south and west, and by the late 19th century the craft had become so popular that a healthy market for pre-stamped designs had developed.

The rug opposite features a cat design adapted from a late-19th-century hooked rug from Lancaster County, Pennsylvania. It is very easy to hook and has an appealing naive quality that results from the simple pattern and the wide strips of fabric used. If you like, you can adapt the directions that follow to hook any simple, linear design—perhaps a child's drawing or a quilt pattern.

◆ IMPORTANT INFORMATION

This 24½ x 33½-inch rug is a traditional hooked rug, worked in the primitive style. In rugmaking, the term "traditional" refers to a method of hooking in which a simple hook is used to pull strips of fabric to form a looped pile. (This differs from latch hooking, in which cut lengths of yarn are knotted onto a backing with a special ratcheting hook.) The term "primitive" refers to a rug in which the strips of fabric used are at least ¼ inch wide.

The rug should be hooked on a durable foundation; the primitive burlap specified is a sturdy, even-weave cloth, which is woven with the same number of threads running lengthwise and crosswise in each square inch. This type of burlap, which has an open mesh large enough to accommodate the ¼-inch fabric strips, is available from rug-making suppliers; it is not the same as the burlap you can purchase at a variety store, which is neither evenly woven nor durable. If you wish to practice hooking to see whether you enjoy it before you invest in the primitive burlap, you can work a sample on burlap of any quality. Rug hooks are available at crafts stores and the notions department of most variety stores.

When selecting the fabric for your rug, choose medium-weight wool. The yardage specified in the materials list on page 84 is the approximate amount of fabric you will need, the exact amount will depend on the fabric weight, the frequency with which you change colors, and your hooking density. The strips must be cut on the straight grain so that they do not stretch when the fabric is hooked. Using a transparent graphed ruler will make measuring and cutting the strips easy.

Most of the fabrics used in this rug are solid-color; some plaids, however, were chosen to create an interesting pattern in the border blocks. You might consider

An entry in an 1839 issue of the Farmer's Monthly Visitor prompted women to make good use of their fabric scraps. "After old coats, pantaloons, etc. have been cut up for boys, and are no longer capable of being converted into garments," advised the author, "cut them into strips, and employ the leisure moments of children or domestics in sewing and braiding them for door-mats."

experimenting with tweeds, checks, and stripes as well. You may also want to vary the shades of your fabrics in the larger, same-color areas. You can mix different fabrics of the same color, or try overdyeing the same fabric to produce a variety of related shades (for information on overdyeing, see page 81).

Before hooking the rug, you will need to enlarge the Scaled Cat Pattern on page 87. Then, referring to the Scaled Schematic Diagram opposite, mark the diagram in full scale onto the burlap. Use a permanent marking pen so that the marks will not bleed and spoil your work if the rug becomes wet. After you mark the burlap, you will need to stretch it on a rug frame. (If you do not have access to a rug frame, which is self-supporting and adjustable, make a 32 x 40-inch frame from canvas stretchers, available at art supply stores.) The burlap must be taut in the frame to ensure an even loop tension. Before cutting the burlap, make sure that it is large enough to fit in your rug frame. If it is not, baste some muslin to the edges to extend them.

The arrows in the Scaled Schematic Diagram indicate the direction in which to hook the rows of loops within different areas; the broken lines indicate a directional area, but not a change in color. These directional changes help create visual interest within a large, single-color space. Small areas should be filled with rows of contour hooking that follow the shape of the area. When outlining, always hook directly over the diagram outline drawn on the burlap. Before you begin, be sure to read all the directions. If you have never hooked a rug, refer to Step 5 in the directions and practice the technique in the burlap border after the burlap is stretched in the frame.

◆ MATERIALS AND EQUIPMENT

1 yard 10-ounce primitive burlap,
  45 inches wide
1 yard green wool fabric, 54 inches wide
  (for background)
¾ yard black wool fabric, 54 inches wide
  (for cats)
Scraps of wool fabric in assorted colors,
  approximately 2 square yards total
  (for border blocks)
Scraps of wool fabric in tan and white
  (for bench and cat details)
10 yards green knitting worsted
3¼ yards twill tape, 2 inches wide
Carpet thread

Rug frame, or canvas stretchers to make
  32 x 40-inch frame
Strip cutter with #8 blade (optional)
#2 primitive rug hook
Clear plastic bags
1 piece graph paper, 11 x 14 inches
Yarn needle
Sewing needle
Transparent graphed ruler
Scissors
Permanent marking pen
Dressmaker's chalk
Dressmaker's pins
Pushpins

◆DIRECTIONS

1. *Cutting the wool strips:* Cut the wool into strips that measure ¼ inch wide and 15 inches long. If you are using a strip cutter (a rugmaking tool designed for cutting the strips in bulk), follow the manufacturer's directions. If you are cutting strips one at a time with scissors, use the ruler and chalk to mark the fabric and cut the strips on the marked lines. Separate the strips according to color and place them in clear plastic bags.

2. *Enlarging the cat pattern:* Using the transparent ruler and a pencil, measure and mark a grid of 1-inch squares onto the graph paper. Referring to the grid in the Scaled Cat Pattern on page 87, mark the outline of the cat in full scale onto your ruled paper. Cut out the cat pattern, and the eyes, nose, and mouth, along the lines.

3. *Marking the burlap:* Using the permanent marking pen, mark a 24 x 33-inch rectangle on the burlap, leaving a generous margin all around. Referring to the measurements in the Scaled Schematic Diagram below, mark the rug pattern within this rectangle. Begin by marking the border of squares, then mark the bench outline. Still referring to the diagram, position the paper cat pattern on the burlap so that the

Scaled Schematic Diagram

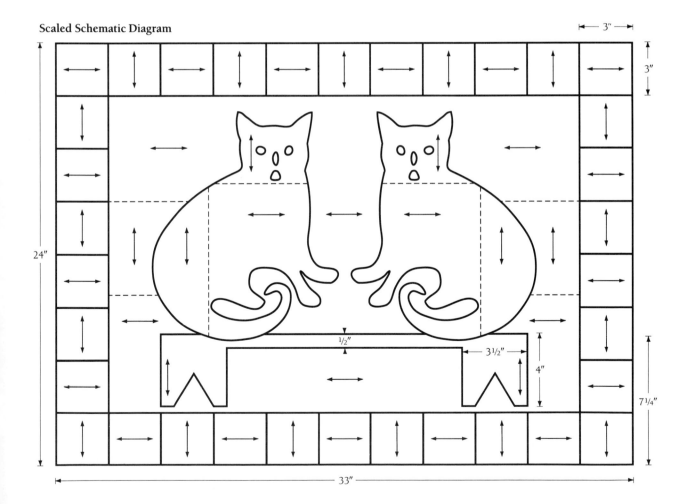

cat sits near the right end of the bench, and trace around the cat. Reverse the paper cat pattern and position it so that the cat sits near the left end of the bench; trace again.

4. *Attaching the burlap to the frame:* Following the manufacturer's directions, attach the burlap to the rug frame, marked side up. If you are using canvas stretchers, attach the burlap with pushpins placed at 1-inch intervals.

5. *Learning to hook:* If you do not know how to hook, practice in a border area of the burlap. Hold the end of one wool strip against the wrong side of the burlap with one hand. Hold the hook in your other hand and, from the right side, insert it through one opening in the weave; grasp the strip and pull the cut end through about ½ inch. Skip two threads on the burlap, insert the hook, and again pull up the strip, making a ¼-inch loop; remove the hook. In this manner, continue to pull loops to the right side of the burlap firmly and evenly (Illustration A). The loops will be held in place by their own density. When you reach the end of a strip, pull it to the right side of the work and trim the excess about ½ inch above the loops.

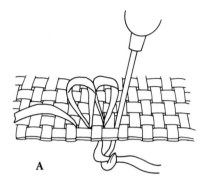

A

6. *Beginning the rug:* Begin by hooking the facial features of the cats with white. Then outline the cats with a row of white loops. Hook a row of black loops just inside the white outlines, then fill in the cats with black, contouring your hooking around the faces, tails, and legs, and hooking the rest of the cats in blocks of horizontal and vertical rows as indicated by the arrows in the Scaled Schematic Diagram. Hook the bench with tan wool.

7. *Filling in the background:* Outline the background area with a row of green loops. Then fill in the green background, as indicated by the arrows in the Scaled Schematic Diagram. Contour your hooking around the legs and tails of the cats.

8. *Hooking the border:* Hook an outline row of green loops all along the outer edge of the rug, then hook a row of green loops between each of the border blocks. Select a color for the upper left block and hook the block in horizontal rows. Select another color for the block immediately below it and hook the block in vertical rows. Hook the remaining blocks, continuing to alternate the direction in which you work, and using any colors you wish.

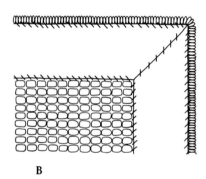

B

9. *Finishing the right side of the rug:* Trim all the cut ends of the strips even with the loops. Remove the rug from the frame. Trim the burlap, leaving a 1½-inch margin around the hooked area. Fold 1¼ inches of the margin to the wrong side and press. With the right side of the rug facing up, and starting wherever you wish, overcast the folded edge, using the yarn needle and a 24-inch length of the knitting worsted. Bring the needle up from the back as close as possible to the outer row of hooking, leaving a 2-inch tail of yarn at the back. Pass the needle over the edge and bring it up again as close as possible to the first stitch; continue in this manner. To end a length of yarn as you overcast, slide the needle under a few stitches on the back and leave a 2-inch tail. (When the entire edge is overcast, turn the rug over and tie together adjacent loose yarn ends; do not trim the excess yarn.)

10. *Hemming the rug:* With the wrong side up, place the rug on a worktable. Fold in the burlap margin at each corner and miter; trim the bulk from under the fold and stitch the fold closed with the carpet thread. Starting anywhere along one side, place the twill tape over the burlap margin and pin in place with one edge against the overcasting. Tuck the loose ends of the yarn under the tape. Fold the twill tape at each corner, miter, and slipstitch. Overlap the ends of the twill tape 1 inch; trim the excess and fold under the end of the upper piece. Slipstitch both edges of the twill tape to the burlap all the way around the rug and remove the pins (Illustration B). ◆

SCALED CAT PATTERN

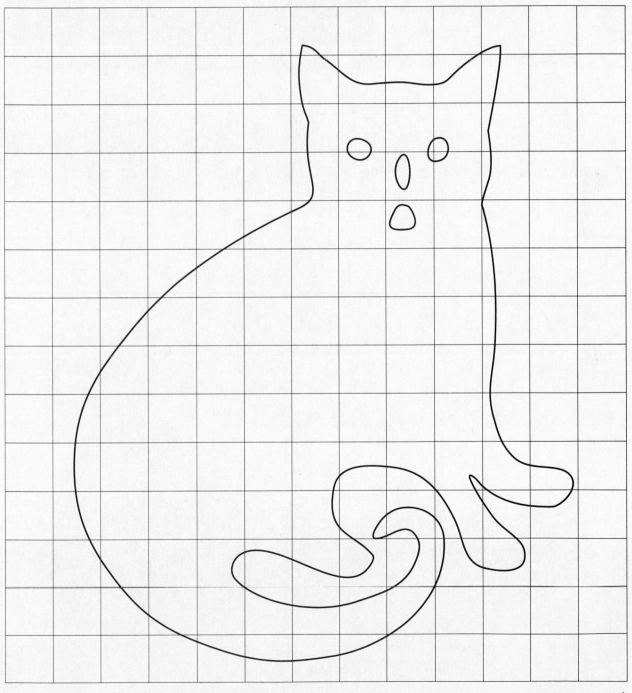

one square = one inch

GRENFELL RUGS

In 1892, Dr Wilfred Grenfell, an English medical missionary and writer, arrived in Labrador, Newfoundland, on a hospital ship. He found that the people in the desolate settlements—icebound most of the year—were dependent entirely on trapping and fishing for their livelihood, and living conditions were bleak. Grenfell decided to stay on, establishing a mission and hospitals, and encouraging the development of local crafts into cottage industries that would generate income for the inhabitants.

Rug hooking became one of the most successful of these industries. Grenfell not only encouraged individuals to create their own designs, but also made kits available to rug hookers through the mission. Much of the fabric used in the rugs was cut from discarded clothing that was gathered and sent to Labrador by English and American volunteers; often the shipments included cotton-knit underwear and silk stockings. The rich dye colors and tight hooking of Grenfell rugs gave them an effect similar to needlepoint.

Production thrived from about 1912 to about 1940, and the rugs hooked in the area during this period were sold widely throughout the United States and England in hotels, resorts, and mission stores. Now known as Grenfell rugs, these rugs (as well as Grenfell mats and bags) are characterized by crisply outlined designs, and typically feature subjects with northern themes, such as polar bears, puffins, and sled-dog teams.

Penny Rug

Probably developed as a way to use wool scraps that were too small to go into braided rugs, penny rugs became fashionable in the middle of the 19th century and continued to be made into the early 1900s. The "pennies"—layered fabric circles—were usually organized into a regular color pattern, and the rugs were made in a variety of geometric shapes; circles, rectangles, octagons, and hexagons were all common. Small rugs, like the antique woolen piece opposite, were often used as table coverings.

◆ IMPORTANT INFORMATION

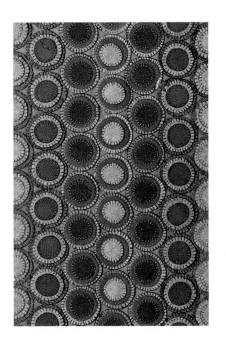

Each penny in this design is made of three circles of fabric layered concentrically and stitched together with buttonhole stitching. The design requires a total of 205 pennies made from eleven colors and layered in six different combinations. Once assembled, the pennies are sewn to a backing in a concentric pattern.

The pennies can be made from medium-weight, firmly woven wool fabrics or from good-quality felt. You can alter the colors on the charts to reflect your own color preferences. When cutting, you can layer the wool to cut several circles at once—but before doing so, test how many layers your scissors will cut through with ease.

To make the pennies, you will need to cut circular templates using the full-size Penny Patterns on page 92, which are labeled with the numbers 3, 2, and 1. In the directions that follow, you will find references to two important charts, a Cutting Chart and a Color Combination Chart; both charts refer to the circle sizes by number, so be sure to label your templates. The Cutting Chart on page 93 indicates how many of each circle you will need to cut from each color, as well as how much fabric is required to do so. The Color Combination Chart on page 93 indicates how to layer the circles in the correct color combinations; the six combinations are designated with the letters A, B, C, D, E, and F. As you make the rug, refer to the Schematic Diagram on page 93 to cut the rug backing and to lay out the pennies. You can work the buttonhole stitch with carpet thread, buttonhole twist, pearl cotton, or embroidery floss. If you plan to use your rug on a floor, carpet thread is recommended.

◆ MATERIALS AND EQUIPMENT

Assorted wool fabrics or felt, for pennies
  (see Cutting Chart on page 93 for amounts)
1 piece wool, 22 x 38 inches, for backing
Carpet thread, buttonhole twist, pearl
  cotton, or embroidery floss
Tracing paper

Lightweight cardboard
T-square
Scissors
Embroidery needle
Dressmaker's pins

Buttonhole Stitch

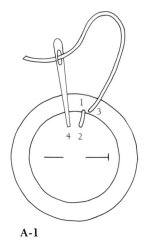

A-1

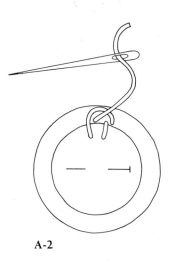

A-2

◆ DIRECTIONS

1. *Making the templates:* Trace the Penny Patterns below onto the tracing paper; cut out. Place the patterns on the cardboard, draw around them, label, and cut out.

2. *Cutting the fabric circles:* Refer to the Cutting Chart opposite to determine how many circles to cut in each size from each color. With the wrong sides up, lay the fabrics on a worktable. Place a circle template on the appropriate fabric, draw around it and cut out. Repeat until you have cut all the circles.

3. *Assembling the pennies:* Refer to the Color Combination chart opposite to assemble the pennies. Center a small circle (Pattern 3) on the appropriately colored medium circle (Pattern 2) and pin. Referring to Illustration A-1, sew the circles together with buttonhole stitch, using the embroidery needle and your choice of thread. To work buttonhole stitch, bring the needle up from the back through the medium circle at the edge of the small circle at point 1. Insert the needle at point 2, ⅛ inch inside the edge of the small circle, and bring it up again in the medium circle at point 3, just to the right of the first stitch. Insert the needle at point 4; as you pull it through, catch a loop of thread with your thumb. Bring the needle back up through the medium circle ⅛ inch to the left of the first stitch, passing it through the loop of thread (Illustration A-2), and pull taut. Continue in this manner around the circle. Remove the pin. Center the stitched double circle on the appropriately colored large circle (Pattern 1); pin and stitch in the same manner. Repeat to make all the pennies.

4. *Preparing the backing:* Using the T-square and a pencil, mark a 21 x 36-inch rectangle on the wrong side of the fabric. Mark a point 6 inches in from each end on each long side. Mark the midpoints of the short sides. Join these points across the four corners. Cut, following the angled lines. Overcast the raw edges of the backing with zigzag or overcast stitching. Baste a center line both lengthwise and crosswise.

5. *Attaching the pennies:* Referring to the Schematic Diagram opposite, pin one F penny onto the center of the backing and stitch it in place using buttonhole stitch; remove the pin. Stitch three F pennies to either side of the center penny on the 36-inch basted line. Stitch an E penny to each end of the row. Position and stitch the remaining E pennies above and below this row, fitting them snugly between the F pennies. Referring to the diagram, continue attaching the pennies in this manner. For the outer band of pennies, start by centering a penny over each corner, then fill in the rest. ◆

PENNY PATTERNS

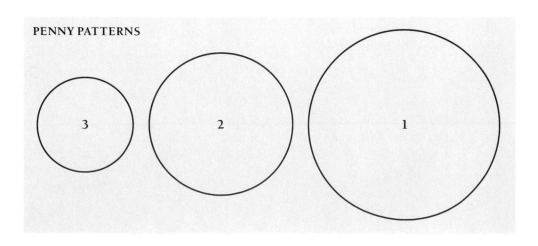

Cutting Chart

color	moss green	dark taupe	light slate	cadet blue	beige	caramel	plum	black	forest green	olive	wine
fabric (inches)	25 x 25	16 x 18	12 x 12	16 x 18	14 x 17	9 x 11	9 x 9	12 x 13	8 x 8	7 x 7	5 x 7
pattern 1	126	54	25								
pattern 2				90	50	30	25				
pattern 3					37			90	36	24	18

Color Combination Chart

penny key	A	B	C	D	E	F
quantity	90	36	30	24	18	7
pattern 1	moss green	moss green	dark taupe	dark taupe	light slate	light slate
pattern 2	cadet blue	beige	caramel	beige	plum	plum
pattern 3	black	forest green	beige	olive	wine	beige

Schematic Diagram

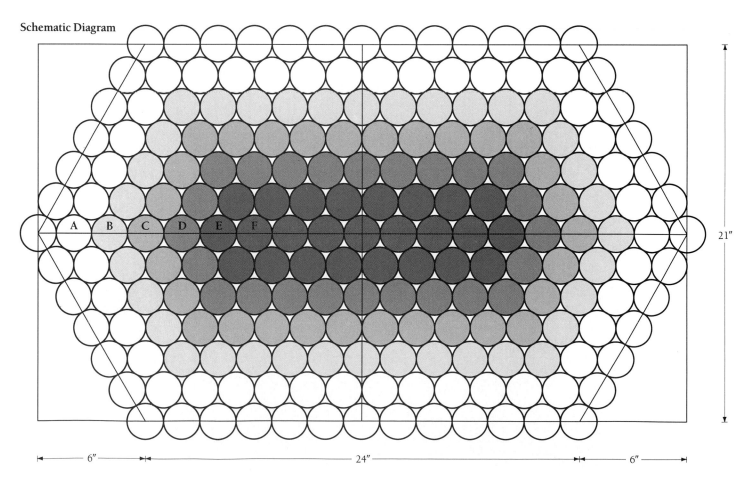

93

Paper Crafting

*decorative cutting,
pasting, and painting*

Paper is a marvelously adaptable material. It comes in many weights, textures, and colors. It can be painted, cut, or used as a covering. And it is also relatively inexpensive, so it is a good medium to work in if you are new to handicrafts.

This chapter shows you how to cut a plain piece of paper into a Pennsylvania-German scherenshnitt picture, and how to cut and pierce paper to produce delicate, translucent lampshade panels. If you fancy cutting up pretty printed papers, you might be interested in the project for making decoupage dresser accessories; in decoupage, imaginatively arranged graphic images can capture a particular mood or sentiment—and you don't have to be able to draw or paint to convey it. Colorful printed papers can also be used to cover bandboxes. And if it is decorated paper that intrigues you, try the project for marbling; the process is tricky, but once you master it, you will be able to produce papers that are works of art in themselves.

*Decorative and useful bandboxes are crafted by putting together simple chipboard
forms and covering them with pretty wallpaper (see pages 110-114).*

Cut-and-Pierced Lampshade

The delicate floral pattern in the paper lampshade opposite is made by the traditional method of cutting and piercing. While the patterns produced by this craft can be quite intricate, the process is very easy to learn. The paper is simply pierced, then cut and curled away from the surface so that the cut-out areas can be clearly seen; none of the paper is cut completely away. You can make a lampshade in the pattern shown here or devise your own pattern, perhaps adapting a design from your wallpaper or upholstery fabrics.

The following decorating tip is from House and Home: A Complete Housewife's Guide, *published in 1889. "I hope you have a reading lamp. There is one in nearly every house now-a-days....Set the lamp invitingly nearer one side of the table than the other, where it will mean something. Scatter around it books that are readable and have been read."*

◆ IMPORTANT INFORMATION

To make this lampshade, you will need to transfer the full-size Lampshade Pattern on page 99 to heavy paper panels. Before the shade is assembled, the panels are pierced, cut, and curled; they are then backed with lining paper and mounted on a wire frame. Don't try using a purchased paper lampshade; it would be awkward to pierce and not worth the trouble, since attaching the paper to a frame is easy. The only special equipment you will need is a lampshade piercer. The piercer has a handle with a different-size piercing needle at each end; the larger needle is used to pierce the large dots in the design, the smaller needle is used to pierce the lines of closely spaced dots.

Before you begin, study the pattern so that you understand the design elements. All the cutting, piercing, and curling is done on the marked side of the paper, which will be the inner side of the shade; as a result, the design you trace will appear in reverse on the finished shade. The six-paneled lampshade shown here measures 5 inches across the top, 12 inches across the bottom, and 7 inches high. The pattern, however, can be adapted for a lampshade of any size. Lampshade piercers, lining paper, and frames are available from lampshade-making suppliers and some crafts stores.

◆ MATERIALS AND EQUIPMENT

6-paneled wire lampshade frame, 7 inches high
1 sheet ecru lampshade paper, 26 x 38 inches
1 sheet white lining paper, 26 x 38 inches
1½ yards ecru grosgrain ribbon, ⅝ inch wide
1½ yards ecru grosgrain ribbon, ⅛ inch wide
1½ yards blue grosgrain ribbon, ⅛ inch wide
Lampshade piercer

Craft knife
Cutting mat
Tracing paper
Artist's transfer paper
Terry cloth towel
Clear-drying craft glue
Scissors
Clothespins

ABOUT PAPER

The word "paper" comes from *Cyperus papyrus*, the name of a water reed that was used to make a paperlike product in ancient Egypt and, later, in Greece and Rome. The reed was cut into long strips, which were laid out in several layers crossing at right angles, and then soaked in water. When the strips had softened, the layers were hammered flat and then dried in the sun, forming a sheet.

A distant relative of papyrus, paper as it is known today is made from plant or cloth fibers that are macerated and mixed with water until they form a fibrous pulp. When the pulp is lifted from the water on screens and allowed to drain, a matted mass remains: when flattened and dried, it becomes a sheet of paper.

Most papers—everything from gift wrap to newsprint—are now made from wood pulp. However, fine grass and fiber, or "rag," papers have been made for centuries from many different plants, including flax, cotton, and hemp, as well as the inner bark of certain trees. In fact, nearly all plant and cloth fibers can produce some sort of paper.

The Chinese are credited with inventing the first "true" paper, made from silk pulp, around the 2nd century A.D. They later found that paper could also be made from bamboo and mulberry. Knowledge of Chinese techniques gradually spread westward along the trade routes to Europe, reaching Spain by the 12th century, and England by the 1400s. Lacking silk and other Oriental plant materials, the Europeans introduced the use of cotton and linen rags for fibers. Cotton is now the fiber most commonly used for rag paper.

Depending on the materials they are made from, papers differ in texture, strength, and absorbency, as well as in color. In some, such as mulberry and cotton papers, leaves, flowers, or long fibers are often added to the pulp for decorative effect. The papers at left, displayed on a sheet of papyrus, are made from the five traditional fibers listed below.

1. Mulberry The soft inner bark of the paper-mulberry tree is traditionally used by the Japanese to make a handsome, fibrous paper. The long mulberry fibers not only are decorative, but give the thin paper strength.

2. Daphne A shrub native to the mountains of Nepal and Bhutan, daphne is used to produce lightweight but strong papers.

3. Linen Linen papers, made from flax fibers, are less absorbent than other types of paper. The crisp surface of the thin, nearly transparent, linen papers is sometimes compared to that of parchment.

4. Cotton The most commonly used fiber for handmade papers is cotton. Tea leaves, sugar cane, feathers, and flowers were mixed into the cotton pulp of these papers to add texture and color.

5. Hemp Hemp-fiber papers, which can range from very thin to a cardboardlike thickness, are extremely strong and absorbent, and surprisingly silky to the touch.

Paper Marbling

Traditionally used in bookbinding, paper marbling, in which paper is decorated with intricate patterns through the use of floating colors, originated in Persia in the 15th century. By the end of the 16th century, the technique was known in Turkey, where finely marbled papers were used for official documents (if the writing was tampered with, the marbling would be disturbed and the fraud revealed). At this time, marbled papers were being exported from the Middle East to Europe, but they were not actually produced there until a hundred years later. France and Germany were the primary Western makers of marbled papers until the middle of the 19th century, when English marblers mastered the art. Loath to reveal the details of the technique, marblers worked in secrecy and their craft was long shrouded in mystery. While the technique is now well known, the patterns, which were developed in prescribed colors and given names, have changed very little over the centuries.

Today, marbled papers are still used in bookbinding as well as to decorate accessories such as picture mats, lampshades, and stationery. They may also be substituted for wallpaper when making the bandboxes shown on pages 110-111.

◆ IMPORTANT INFORMATION

Paper marbling is an unpredictable process and you should expect your first marbling attempts to have mixed results; experience will give you a true understanding of the materials and techniques. The outcome is affected by room temperature and humidity, dust, water quality, and the brand of colors used. For best results, the temperature in your workroom should be about 65 degrees and should remain constant. (If the air is very dry, you may need to use a humidifier.) Be sure to read all the directions before starting so that you understand how the work progresses, and set aside plenty of time. The materials and equipment mentioned are available from marbling suppliers and some art supply stores.

In paper marbling, paints or colored inks are dropped onto a viscous bath to create a pattern, and a piece of paper treated with alum (aluminum potassium sulfate) is then laid onto the floating colors; when the paper is lifted away, the pattern adheres to it. The bath, called size, is made from a mixture of water and carrageenin, a thickening agent. The size should be mixed in a proportion of 2 tablespoons of carrageenin per gallon of water and poured into a trough to a depth of about 1 inch. As the size sits, a skin tends to form on its surface and must be skimmed off just before the colors are dropped on.

For the colors, you can use marbling ink, acrylic paint, or gouache—a type of opaque watercolor. Each of these is water-soluble; gouache, however, may be tricky to use. The colors are mixed with ox gall, a dispersing agent, before they are dropped onto the size; the ox gall allows the colors to spread and keeps them from blending together, while the viscosity of the size supports the colors.

Bandboxes

During the first half of the 19th century, bandboxes like those at left were particularly popular in America and were commonly used both as luggage and as storage for a varied assortment of personal effects. These versatile containers were made of wood or cardboard, and were invariably covered with bright, block-printed wallpapers. Many of the distinctive paper designs, which might depict landmarks, famous people, classical motifs, or floral patterns, were created by manufacturers specifically for the box exteriors; the interiors, by contrast, were usually lined with bits and pieces of discarded newspaper. These handsome and colorful boxes are easy to make and can serve as pretty storage containers for all manner of treasures.

◆ IMPORTANT INFORMATION

The bandboxes shown here are made from chipboard—a thin paper board similar to poster board—and then covered with wallpaper and lined with newspaper. Each bandbox is made from four chipboard pieces: the box bottom, the box body, the lid top, and the lid lip. The size of the bottom determines the sizes of the three other pieces and of the wallpaper covering. Chipboard, available at art supply stores, is sold in single, double, and triple thicknesses; use the double-thickness board to make the box bottom and lid top, and the single-thickness board, which is more flexible, to make the box body and lid lip.

When marking the pattern onto the wallpaper, be sure to consider the position of any one-way designs or dominant motifs; double-check their placement when pasting the paper onto the box. You will need approximately 1 square yard of wallpaper; the exact amount will depend on the scale of the designs or motifs. Using a transparent graphed ruler will make measuring the pieces easy.

To cover the box, you can use regular wallpaper and wallpaper paste, or prepasted wallpaper. In either case, follow the manufacturer's directions; if you are using prepasted paper, dampen it when the directions on pages 112-113 specify to apply paste. To prevent the chipboard from warping, be careful not to overdampen the wallpaper. Be sure to smooth out any air bubbles with your fingers when applying the paper to the chipboard. Before assembling the pieces, you should paste a scrap of wallpaper to a scrap of the chipboard so that you can get a feel for the process. Always let the paper set for at least one hour before handling.

The directions that follow are for making a bandbox measuring 9 x 7 x 6¾ inches using the largest of the oval Bandbox Bottom Patterns on page 114. The two smaller patterns are provided for your convenience, should you desire to make smaller bandboxes. To make these smaller boxes, simply follow the same procedure you would for making the large bandbox; the height of the box, however, can vary as you choose. To make a round box, draw a circular pattern with a compass.

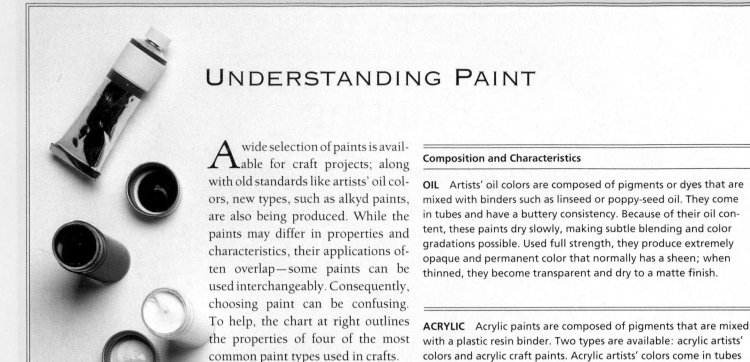

UNDERSTANDING PAINT

A wide selection of paints is available for craft projects; along with old standards like artists' oil colors, new types, such as alkyd paints, are also being produced. While the paints may differ in properties and characteristics, their applications often overlap—some paints can be used interchangeably. Consequently, choosing paint can be confusing. To help, the chart at right outlines the properties of four of the most common paint types used in crafts.

When purchasing paint, keep in mind that different brands of the same type of paint are not identical in quality and characteristics. Acrylic craft paint made by one company, for example, may be quicker drying or thicker than an acrylic craft paint produced by another manufacturer. Colors of the same name also vary in appearance.

Composition and Characteristics

OIL   Artists' oil colors are composed of pigments or dyes that are mixed with binders such as linseed or poppy-seed oil. They come in tubes and have a buttery consistency. Because of their oil content, these paints dry slowly, making subtle blending and color gradations possible. Used full strength, they produce extremely opaque and permanent color that normally has a sheen; when thinned, they become transparent and dry to a matte finish.

ACRYLIC   Acrylic paints are composed of pigments that are mixed with a plastic resin binder. Two types are available: acrylic artists' colors and acrylic craft paints. Acrylic artists' colors come in tubes and can easily be mixed for a versatile range of colors. Acrylic craft paints come in small jars and are more liquid than acrylic artists' colors; some brands are available premixed in "country" colors. Both types produce a permanent and relatively opaque color; when mixed with water, they become transparent.

ALKYD   Alkyd artists' colors are composed of pigments that are mixed with an alkyd (alcohol and acid) resin and an oil binder. They come in tubes, have the consistency of oil colors, and can be mixed with oil colors. Alkyd paints dry more quickly than oil paints but more slowly than acrylic paints, and they produce a permanent color that is brighter than either.

JAPAN   Japan colors are composed of ground pigments that are mixed in a resinous varnish containing little or no oil. The paints come in both tubes and jars, and are available in a wide variety of colors. For an even broader color range, they can be mixed with oil paint, but the oil will slow down the drying time. Japan colors dry with a flat, opaque appearance.

Uses	Advantages	Disadvantages
◆ Oil colors can be used on many materials, including canvas, wood, metal, porcelain, and glass. They are generally not recommended for stenciling because they dry slowly.	◆ Oil colors are excellent for small-scale, decorative painting because they are opaque and fine textured. Oils can be mixed to produce a wide range of colors.	◆ Oil colors can take days to dry (different colors dry at different rates), and require the use of flammable solvents such as turpentine for thinning and cleanup. Some oil colors contain lead.
◆ Acrylic paints can be used on canvas, wood, paper, and metal; sand and prime metal surfaces before painting. Acrylic craft paints are the easiest acrylic paints to use for stenciling.	◆ Acrylic paints dry in a few minutes and require only water for thinning and cleanup. Once dry, the paints remain flexible, so painted fabrics can be rolled or folded without cracking the colors.	◆ Subtle blending of colors is difficult because acrylics dry quickly. Although they are water-soluble when wet, the paints are extremely hard to remove from brushes if allowed to dry.
◆ Alkyd artists' colors can be used on canvas, wood, glass, metal, and porcelain. They can also be used for wall stenciling.	◆ Alkyd artists' colors dry thoroughly in less than a day, but remain mixable on a palette for several hours. All alkyd artists' colors dry at the same rate and to the same degree of gloss.	◆ Alkyd colors require the use of flammable solvents such as turpentine or mineral spirits for thinning and cleanup.
◆ Japan colors have traditionally been used for American decorative painting. They are especially suitable for stenciling on furniture and walls, and for detailed work on wood or metal.	◆ The varnish base makes Japan colors extremely quick drying. The paints produce a flat color that can be shaded or glazed for a wide variety of effects.	◆ Japan colors can be difficult to find. They require flammable solvents such as turpentine and mineral spirits for thinning and cleanup.

UNDERSTANDING BRUSHES

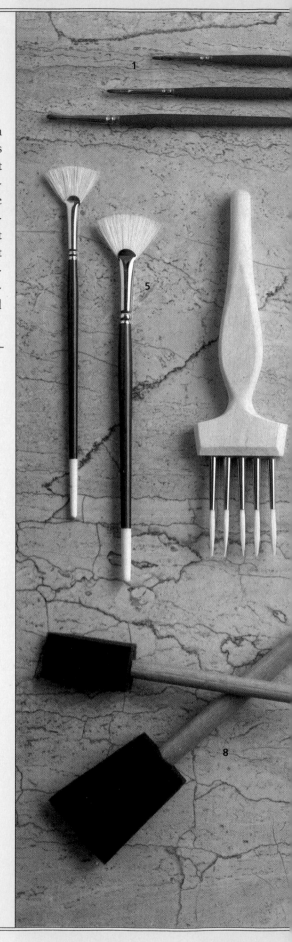

Brushes are designed for dozens of specific uses. In addition to a wide range of artists' brushes, there are brushes created especially for particular projects like grain-painting and stenciling. Shown here are some of the basic brushes used in crafts. Most are available with either natural or synthetic bristles in various grades. Synthetic brushes are used with acrylic paints because the medium can erode natural bristles.

Brushes like those listed are often made with high-quality materials and they can be expensive. It is best to start out with only the basic brushes required for a project: purchase others only as you become more advanced and are ready to experiment with new techniques. Buy the best quality brush you can afford. A well-made brush will provide better control, and properly cared for, it should last for years.

1. Brights   Characterized by flat, short bristles with squared ends, these brushes can be used with buttery paints such as oils, and fluid paints like watercolors. In decorative painting, brights are used for filling in areas of color.

2. Stencil brushes   Made with blunt-cut natural hog bristles, stencil brushes are used for applying paint through a stencil. The brushes produce a softly textured, stippled effect, and the blunt bristles help prevent the paint from seeping under the edge of the stencil.

3. Badger softeners   Large badger-hair brushes are used dry to soften colors and blend brushstrokes in oil and watercolor painting. They are also used in grain-painting to produce thin washes of color and grain-like striations.

4. Rounds   Round brushes, available in a wide range of sizes, are best used with fluid paints. The flexible bristles and pointed tip can produce fine lines, as well as the "comma strokes" often used in decorative painting.

5. Fans   Fan brushes are used dry to blend colors in oil and acrylic painting. A variety of large fan brushes is also available for similar use in grain-painting.

6. Overgrainers   Overgrainers are used for applying a dark "wood grain" or other precise detail on a dry, previously grained surface.

7. Liners   Liners are designed to make smooth, flowing brushstrokes such as those used for scrollwork and script. The long, tapered bristles hold a lot of paint and therefore require less dipping than other brushes.

8. Sponge brushes   Inexpensive, disposable brushes made of sponge are adequate for applying a base color to a surface. They can be used with all paint types but will dissolve if cleaned in turpentine or mineral spirits.

9. Brights   See (1) above.

10. Stipplers   Stipplers are used for making decorative finishes. Used dry on a freshly painted surface, the bristles lift flecks of color to create a freckled or lightly mottled surface.

Country Floor Cloth

Painted canvas cloths were probably among the first types of floor coverings used in this country. Whether they were store-bought or made at home, such cloths had many attributes: they provided good insulation, they were washable, and they were durable, requiring only an occasional coat of varnish for upkeep. Easy to make, they are still popular today. (For more floor cloth design ideas, see pages 132-133.)

◆ IMPORTANT INFORMATION

This floor cloth, which measures about 33 x 41 inches, is made of cotton duck canvas. After the canvas is primed with gesso, it is marked in pencil with a 2-inch grid. By referring to the Scaled Schematic Diagram on page 130, you will be able to mark the diamond and checkerboard pattern directly onto this grid.

The design is applied in acrylic craft paint and is sealed with polyurethane for protection. Before painting, the yellow and teal diamonds are masked off with tape, which is sealed with acrylic matte medium to prevent bleeding. The checkerboard border is painted with two simple stencils cut from stencil acetate, a clear plastic film.

After priming the canvas, let the gesso dry for at least two hours. Let the acrylic paint set a few moments before moving the stencils, and be sure the paint is dry to the touch before masking over it or applying adjacent colors. When you seal the tape, let the acrylic matte medium dry for half an hour before painting over it. Use disposable plastic dishes to hold your paints, and choose an appropriate-size brush for the area you are painting; change or clean brushes when changing colors. The materials and equipment you will need are available at art supply and crafts stores.

The first canvas floor cloths in this country were imported from England, but Americans were manufacturing their own by the late 18th century. In 1793, Joseph Barrell, a wealthy Bostonian, wrote to his London agent and canceled his order for floor cloths "as I find I can supply myself better here."

◆ MATERIALS AND EQUIPMENT

1 piece #10 cotton duck canvas, 36 x 44 inches	*Rolling pin*
1 pint gesso	*Craft knife*
Acrylic craft paint, one 8-ounce container	*Cutting mat*
each in cream, yellow, teal, black, and red	*Scissors*
1 quart clear polyurethane	*Graph paper*
Assorted flat paintbrushes, ¾ to 3 inches	*T-square*
Stencil brushes, 1½ and ½ inches in	*Masking tape, 1 inch wide*
diameter	*Disposable plastic dishes*
Acrylic matte medium	*Paper towels*
White craft glue	*Sandpaper, 150 grit*
1 sheet stencil acetate, 8½ x 11 inches	*Marking pen*
2-quart mixing bowl	*Ruler*

FLOOR CLOTH DESIGNS

In the 18th and 19th centuries, canvas floor cloths were often painted to imitate costly tiling or Oriental carpets. In making your own floor cloth, you may want to reproduce a traditional tile or carpet design, or take a cue from the past to devise a new pattern of your own.

The new floor cloths shown here—painted both freehand and with stencils—were inspired by many different sources, including a Baby Blocks quilt pattern, an antique hooked rug, and the familiar rabbit motif that appears on Dedham pottery. The trompe l'oeil cat on the "Oriental" rug is a contemporary twist on a traditional idea. Let these designs spark your imagination once you have learned how to paint the country floor cloth on page 128.

GRAPHIC GAME BOARDS

The checkerboards above include, clockwise from top left, a c. 1850 board with a sawtooth border, a late-1800s piece with a grain-painted grid, a c. 1880 board painted for a three-dimensional effect, and a Victorian board with gold detailing.

In the days before radio and television, handmade game boards like those designed for checkers, above, and for pachisi, opposite, could be found in almost any household. While some game boards were simply painted, others were distinguished by ingenious graphics and beautifully rendered images; carefully designed and decorated, the finest boards are now considered true folk art by collectors.

Part of the pleasure of looking at early game boards lies in discover-

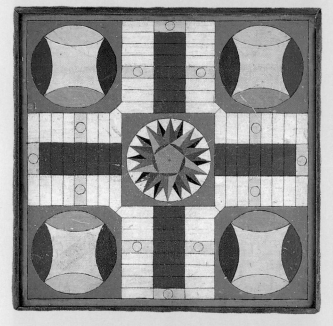
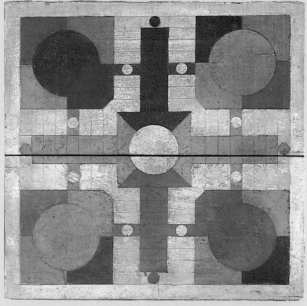
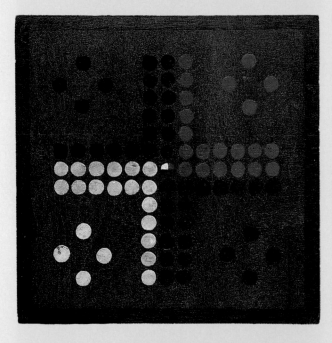

ing the small details that the makers thought to include. Pachisi boards, for instance, sometimes display an elaborate painted landscape or compass rose in the center. Many checkerboards feature trompe l'oeil painting and intricate borders. On some examples, the squares were numbered so that players could carry on a game long distance by penny postcard. The boards shown here date from the 19th and early 20th centuries. Let their striking designs inspire you to create your own.

The pachisi boards above include, clockwise from top left, a late-1800s board with a compass rose motif, a late-1800s two-piece board, an early-1900s board with a checkerboard on the back, and a 1915 piece from Kennebunk, Maine.

Crafting Natural Materials

*working with wood, flowers,
and foliage*

Whether collected on walks through the countryside or purchased through florists or lumberyards, natural materials like those used for the craft projects in this chapter are appealing because they provide a link to the out-of-doors. There is also something very fulfilling in working with these materials: in enjoying the scent of wood and flowers, and in fashioning branches into rustic accessories.

You might want to begin with the dried-flower wreath; it is an easy project that makes a lovely gift. You can purchase flowers already dried or learn to dry them yourself following the directions provided. Or, look to your back yard or nearby woods for branches and twigs suitable for making the twig picture frame; this frame looks just right with a vintage print or photograph. The three other woodworking projects include a bird feeder, a Shaker-style peg-rack shelf, and a primitive Noah's ark that is sure to please the young at heart. While the feeder and ark require some woodworking experience, the shelf is a good project on which to begin learning this skill.

Dried flowers, taped into bunches, are attached to a wreath form (see pages 158-161).

Twig Picture Frame

The picture frame opposite recalls the twig pieces used to furnish the "great camps" and cottages that proliferated in the Adirondack Mountain region of New York State from the 1870s into the 1930s. As America became increasingly industrialized in the decades following the Civil War, many city dwellers yearned for a simpler life and fled to the Adirondacks each summer to pursue the pleasures of nature. Here, rustic resort homes were built from rough-hewn logs and the rooms appointed with furniture and accessories crafted locally from twigs and branches.

*"To the modern man in the
Adirondacks, the roar of the
rapids, the gaunt dead trees
around the lake.... are
sources of joy and refreshment
unspeakable," wrote Henry
Beers in the article "The
Modern Feeling for Nature,"
published in 1904 in* Points
at Issue. *"He sees in them
the unconsciousness, the spon-
taneity, the coarse health of
the great mother from whom
we all are sprung, to whom we
all return, but whose existence
we have forgotten
in the cities."*

◆ IMPORTANT INFORMATION

The directions that follow are for a frame with an opening that measures 13½ inches wide and 16½ inches high, but they can be adapted to any size frame. You will need small branches and twigs in a variety of diameters; refer to the Cutting Chart on page 149 for the sizes that were used for this frame. (If you make a frame that is considerably larger or smaller, adjust the branch and twig sizes accordingly.)

Making a frame out of branches and twigs is by necessity an inexact and creative process. Since no two branches or twigs are identical, just try to find pieces that have approximately the same diameters as the pieces specified in the Cutting Chart. When you gather your wood, choose pieces that appeal to you, and don't look for perfection; the knobs, knots, and bark will give the finished frame character. This frame was made from birch, but beech, ash, oak, ironwood, maple, and hickory would also be good choices, as all of them have pretty bark.

You will need to refer to the Assembly Diagram on page 149 to put the pieces together. The main section of the frame is made of four branches, measuring about 1½ inches in diameter, that are notched to fit together where they cross. After the main section is assembled, a lower bar is added, then decorative twig fretwork is applied to the bottom, sides, and top of the frame. Do not cut the fretwork pieces until the main frame and lower bar are assembled. Be sure to fit all the fretwork pieces for each section before you attach any of them, adjusting until you like the overall effect.

To prevent the pieces from splitting as they are nailed together, you will need to predrill holes through the intersecting pieces. Keep an assortment of galvanized nails on hand; as you work, select a nail for each notched joint that is just a little shorter than the combined thickness of the two pieces being joined. Use a drill bit the same size as the nail you plan to use, and drill each hole to a depth that measures about three-quarters of the length of the nail.

You will need only a few tools to make the frame. Use a crosscut handsaw to cut the branches. Use a coping saw to taper the branch ends, to cut the smaller twigs, and to bevel the ends of the angled twigs.

◆ MATERIALS AND EQUIPMENT

Assorted small branches and twigs (see
Cutting Chart on page 149 for
approximate dimensions)
Galvanized flathead nails, #4p, #6p,
#8p, and #12p
Stain or paint of your choice

Crosscut handsaw
Coping saw
Wood chisel
Drill with selection of bits
Hammer
Ruler

◆ DIRECTIONS

1. *Cutting the branches:* Referring to the Cutting Chart and the Assembly Diagram opposite, cut·two branch pieces for the two side bars (pieces #1), and three branch pieces for the top bar and two bottom bars (pieces #2).

2. *Laying out the main frame:* Arrange the two side bars (pieces #1) and a top and bottom bar (pieces #2) so that they frame an opening that measures 13½ inches wide and 16½ inches long. Using a pencil, on the side, top, and bottom branches make marks for notches where the branches cross.

3. *Cutting the notches:* Using the crosscut handsaw, cut a notch between the markings on each branch piece and chisel out with the hammer and chisel; each notch should be as deep as half the diameter of the branch. Fit the pieces together (Illustration A), adjusting the size of the notches if necessary.

4. *Tapering the branch ends:* Choose one side of the frame to be the front, and place the frame with the front side up on a worktable. Center the lower bar (the remaining, unnotched piece #2) across the bottom of the frame, abutting the ends of the side bars. On the front side of the five framing pieces, make a pencil mark 2 inches in from each exposed branch end. Disassemble the frame and, using the coping saw, taper each piece from the pencil marks to the ends.

5. *Assembling the main frame:* Reassemble the notched pieces and, with the back side up, place the frame on the worktable. Drill a hole through a notched intersection; do not penetrate more than halfway through the lower branch. Hammer a nail into the hole. Repeat for the three other notched intersections.

6. *Attaching the lower bar:* Reposition the lower bar across the bottom of the frame. Drill a hole through the lower bar into the end of each side bar. Hammer a nail into each drill hole.

7. *Cutting, fitting, and laying out the lower fretwork:* With the front side up, place the frame on the worktable. Referring to the Cutting Chart and the Assembly Diagram, cut, fit, and lay out the fretwork twigs between the lower bars of the frame, beveling the ends as needed. For each end of each twig, select a nail long enough to go through the adjacent bar and a short way into the twig. To find the best place to make the drill hole, lay the nail perpendicularly across the bar and over the intersecting twig, and mark the corresponding spot on the bar with a pencil dot.

8. *Attaching the lower fretwork:* Referring to the Assembly Diagram, stand the

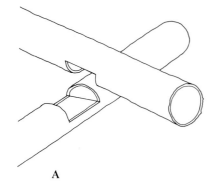

A

frame upright, hold the center twig (piece #3) in place and drill down through the upper bar into it. Hammer a nail into the hole. Turn the frame over and drill through the lower bar into the other end of the twig. In the same manner, attach the diagonal twigs (pieces #4 and #5) to the bars.

9. *Cutting, fitting, laying out, and attaching the upper fretwork:* Referring to the Cutting Chart and the Assembly Diagram, cut, fit, and lay out the fretwork twigs at the top of the frame, beveling the ends as needed. Mark the pieces for nail placement as in Step 7. Start with the center twig (piece #6), then fit in the diagonal twigs (pieces #7 and #8); drill and nail up through the top bar into the bottoms of the twigs. Fit in the horizontal twigs (pieces #9); from the top, drill and nail them at an angle to the center diagonal twigs (pieces #7). Drill and nail through the side bars into the tops of the end diagonal twigs (pieces #8) and into the ends of the horizontal twigs (pieces #9).

10. *Cutting, fitting, laying out, and attaching the side fretwork:* Referring to the Cutting Chart and the Assembly Diagram, cut, fit, and lay out the fretwork twigs (pieces #10, #11, and #12) at the sides of the frame, beveling the ends as needed. Mark the pieces for nail placement as in Step 7. Working from the center twig out, attach the twigs to one side of the frame, drilling and nailing through them into the bars. Repeat for the other side. Stain or paint the tapered ends of the branches. ◆

Cutting Chart

piece #	quantity required	approximate diameter and length			
		½" d.	¾" d.	1" d.	1½" d.
1	2				31"
2	3				26½"
3	1			5"	
4	2		6"		
5	2		6½"		
6	1			7½"	
7	2		10½"		
8	2	3½"			
9	2		5½"		
10	2	3"			
11	4	6"			
12	4	4"			

Assembly Diagram

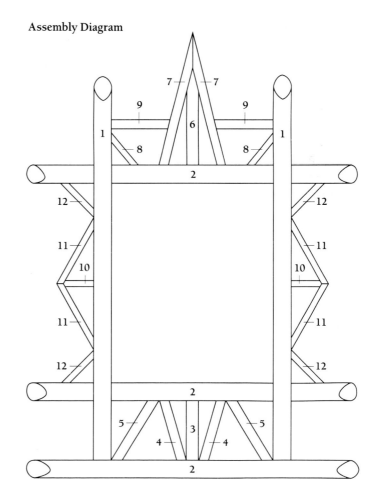

Rustic Tray Bird Feeder

This rustic tray bird feeder is not only simple to build, but is also practical: the wide seed tray makes it easy for birds to land, and they can grip the rough bark to establish a good perch while feeding. Ideally, feeders should be placed on the south or east side of a house, out of the path of cold north and northwest winds. (For more information on feeding feathered friends, see page 153.)

◆ IMPORTANT INFORMATION

This bird feeder, which measures about 6 inches wide, 10 inches long, and 8 inches high, is made from slabs of wood cut from firewood logs, small branches, and a piece of ½-inch pine for the floor. Since no two logs or branches are identical, just try to find pieces that have approximately the same diameters as the pieces specified in the materials list below. Choose logs with thick, sculptural bark for the sides and roof, and small branches with smooth bark for the roof supports.

You will need to refer to the Assembly Diagram on page 152 as you cut and construct the bird feeder. You will need a band saw to "rip" (cut with the grain) the wood to the proper size. (A band saw is a potentially dangerous tool and should only be used by someone who knows how to operate it safely.) To prevent the pieces from splitting as they are screwed together, you will need to predrill holes through the intersecting pieces. Use galvanized drywall screws to attach the pieces. Do not stain, paint, or varnish the interior of the bird feeder.

A contributor to Good Housekeeping's Discovery Book, *published in 1905, suggested scattering crusts and scraps to feed birds, who "congregate each morning, and if breakfast is tardy announce by impatient twitterings that they at least have kept their engagement."*

◆ MATERIALS AND EQUIPMENT

A few pieces firewood, 5½ and 8 inches in diameter, cut into 10-inch lengths
A few branches, 1¼ inches in diameter (enough to cut four 5-inch lengths)
1 branch, 1¾ inches in diameter, 10 inches long
1 branch, ¾ inch in diameter, 10 inches long

1 piece ½-inch pine board, 4½ x 8¾ inches
Band saw
Drill with bits, ⅛ inch and #2 Phillips
Galvanized drywall screws, #6 x 1⅝ inches
Large screw eye
Ruler

◆ DIRECTIONS

1. *Cutting the tray sides and ends:* Referring to Illustration A, use the ruler and a pencil to mark a 4-inch line across one end of one of the 5½-inch-diameter logs. Using the band saw, rip down the length of the log at this mark to make a 10-inch-long section that measures about ¾ inch high at its center. Mark the center of the 4-inch edge on one end and rip down the length of the piece at this mark; these two pieces will be the tray sides (pieces #1). Rip down the log to make another section in the same measurements, and cut a 4½-inch-long piece from it. Rip this section in half lengthwise in the same manner as for the sides; these two pieces will be the tray ends (pieces #2).

2. *Assembling the tray:* Referring to the Assembly Diagram below, place the piece of pine for the tray bottom (piece #3) on a worktable. With the bark side out and the wider edge down, place one of the tray ends (piece #2) at one end of the tray bottom. On the tray end, make a mark 1 inch in from each end and ¼ inch up from the bottom edge. Using the ⅛-inch bit, drill through the tray end into the tray bottom at each mark. Using the #2 Phillips bit, insert a screw into each hole. Repeat to attach the other tray end. In the same manner, attach the tray sides to the bottom, drilling and inserting screws at the centers and the ends.

3. *Making and attaching the roof supports:* From the 1¼-inch-diameter branches, cut four 5-inch-long pieces for the roof supports (pieces #4). Turn the tray on its side and place one support in one corner of the inside of the tray. Drill through the bottom of the tray into the center of the support and insert a screw into the hole. Repeat to attach a roof support at each of the three remaining corners of the tray bottom.

4. *Cutting the triangular roof braces:* Use the ruler and pencil to mark a 1¼-inch line across one end of the 1¾-inch-diameter branch. Using the band saw, rip down the length of the branch at this mark and discard the smaller piece. Cut the remaining section into two 5-inch-long pieces (pieces #5). On the bark side of one piece, mark the center and cut at an angle from the mark out to each end of the piece. Repeat for the other piece.

5. *Cutting the roof:* Referring to Illustration A, use the ruler and pencil to mark a 6-inch line across one end of one of the 7½-inch-diameter logs. Using the band saw, rip down the length of the log at this mark to make a 10-inch-long section that measures about 1½ inches high at its center. Mark the center of the 6-inch edge on one end of the section and rip down the length of the section at this mark to make two quarter-round pieces for the roof (pieces #6).

6. *Attaching the roof braces:* Referring to the Assembly Diagram, place the tray on the worktable with the bottom down. At one end, place the flat bottom side of one triangular roof brace across the roof supports. Drill through the top of the roof brace into each support and insert a screw into each hole. Repeat to attach the second roof brace.

7. *Attaching the roof and ridgepole:* Referring to the Assembly Diagram, slant one of the roof pieces over the roof braces with the 3-inch flat side down and the tapered edge out. Drill a hole through the roof into the center of each brace and insert a screw into each hole. Repeat to attach the second roof piece. Using the ¾-inch-diameter branch for a ridgepole (piece #7), place it in the space between the two roof pieces. At each end, drill a hole through the ridgepole into the top of the roof brace and insert a screw into the hole. Screw the screw eye into the center of the ridgepole. ◆

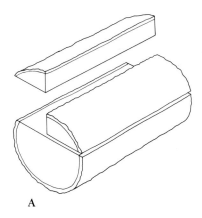

A

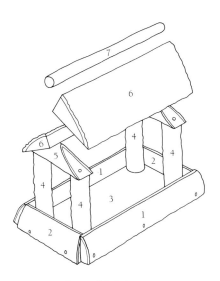

Assembly Diagram

FOR THE BIRDS

While nature offers birds an ample food supply, putting out seed and other treats in your yard will provide a welcome supplement to their diet. From one part of the country to another, nearly all birds of the same species eat the same foods. By understanding what certain species like to eat, you may be able to attract a wide variety of birds to your yard—and derive hours of pleasure from watching them dine at your bird feeder.

Among the most nutritious and popular bird feeds are black-stripe— and the smaller black-oil—sunflower seeds. Sunflower seeds are particular favorites of cardinals, nuthatches, grosbeaks, finches, and chickadees. (Because some birds will scatter other seeds out of a feeder in favor of sunflower seeds, you may want to put your sunflower seeds in a separate feeder.)

Niger (thistle) seed will attract redpolls, goldfinches, and siskins. Peanut hearts are favored by blue jays and tufted titmice. Ground-feeding species, such as juncos, sparrows, doves, pheasants, and quail, prefer cracked corn and white proso millet.

In the winter, suet, and peanut butter mixed with seed, will help add necessary calories to a bird's diet. Suet is especially appealing to nuthatches, woodpeckers, and chickadees. Chopped apples, oranges, and raisins are regarded as treats by tanagers, mockingbirds, orioles, and robins.

Keep in mind that water is also essential to birds. If you feed them, you should provide them with a source of fresh, clean water to quench their thirst.

HOME-DRIED FLOWERS

By drying flowers and foliage yourself, you can take advantage of the widest possible range of plants for use in projects like the dried-flower wreath on pages 158-161. Flowers suitable for drying can be picked from your garden or from along the roadside throughout the growing season. Look for plants that have not yet reached peak bloom; if the blossoms are fully opened, they are likely to lose their petals as they dry. Flowers should be picked on dry days, and they should be examined for insects before being brought indoors.

You should always preserve more flowers than you think you will need, since dried flowers are brittle and can break when handled. Dried flowers also fade readily, so they should be stored away from daylight; they can be packed loosely in layers in covered boxes with tissue between the layers until you are ready to use them. Even in the best of circumstances, however, dried flowers will fade once they are displayed, so plan to replace them with a freshly dried supply about once a year.

The following two pages describe four of the most popular methods for drying flowers at home. Although many types of flowers can be preserved successfully with any of the four methods, others respond better to one technique than to another. A little trial-and-error testing may be necessary before you achieve satisfactory results.

FLOWER DRYING METHODS

AIR-DRYING (I)

Hanging flowers upside down to air-dry is a simple procedure that is suitable for a wide variety of plants, and it is particularly useful if you need to dry large quantities of flowers. The most important requirement is a warm, dark, well-ventilated place in which to hang the plants. Attics and closets are ideal; kitchens should be avoided because moisture and grease would cause dust to stick to the flowers. Well-lit rooms can be used if the flowers are carefully wrapped with paper or enclosed in paper bags to prevent fading. The flowers can be hung from rafters, closet poles, blanket racks, or even coat hangers.

When you cut flowers for hanging, remove any thorns, as well as the lower leaves on the stalks, while the plants are fresh and still easy to strip: once the flowers are tied into bunches and hung to dry, the lower leaves can trap moisture and cause mildew to form on the stems.

Flowers dry at different rates of time, depending on their thickness and moisture content, so similar types should be grouped together when hung. For flowers with many layers of petals, such as roses, limit each bunch to three to five stems; smaller, less dense flowers, like lavender or statice, can be gathered in bunches of eight to ten stems. (The larger the bunch, the longer it will take to dry.) As you form each bunch, stagger the arrangement of stems so that the flower heads will not press together. Bind the stems loosely with a rubber band, then gently fan them apart so that air can circulate around the leaves and flower heads. Attach a loop of string or wire to the bound end and hang the bunches, upside down, leaving at least six inches between them. Most flowers will air-dry in two to five weeks; when the plants are thoroughly dried, the petals and stems will be crisp to the touch.

Because dried flowers are fragile it is best to handle them as little as possible: if space allows, leave the flowers hanging until you are ready to use them.

AIR-DRYING (II)

Air-drying flowers on a flat surface is a straightforward technique that is especially good for preserving varieties that have broad, flat flower heads—Queen Anne's lace, zinnias, and daisies, for example. It is also the most convenient way to dry petals and buds for potpourri. (You will need a warm, dry, well-ventilated place to work.)

A window screen suspended between two chairs makes a good surface for drying the small flower heads and petals for potpourri. When spreading the flowers and petals on the screen be careful not to let them overlap, or moisture will be trapped, causing rot. For large flowers, use screening with an open mesh and pull the stems through (the mesh should still be fine enough to fully support the petals on the surface).

If you do not have room to lay the flowers out flat, try air-drying small flowers on a piece of cheesecloth or muslin that has been hung like a hammock. For large flowers, insert the stems through a caned chair seat or the open weave of a hanging basket. Plants and grasses with sturdy stalks and small flower heads can also be dried upright, supported in a vase or other container.

SAND OR CORNMEAL

Drying flowers in sand or a mixture of cornmeal and borax produces fresher-looking blossoms than the air-drying methods. However, it also requires some patience and practice.

With this technique, flowers are buried in the drying medium, which supports the petals in natural positions while they dry. If you use sand, it must be extremely fine and clean. Fine beach sand should be rinsed well to remove any salt, and thoroughly dried before use. Cornmeal mixtures used for drying can vary; a combination of three parts cornmeal to one part borax is reliable. You will also need sturdy, open containers such as shoe boxes or baking pans. It is best to use a

separate
container for each
type of flower since drying times
differ for the various blossoms.

When using this method, roses and other flowers with dense layers of petals should be dried with the heads upward; their stems, therefore, must be trimmed while the flowers are still fresh. You will need a pair of scissors, and some 22- or 24-gauge florist's wire cut into 6- to 8-inch lengths. Trim each stem to within an inch of the flower, then insert a wire, taking care not to let it poke through the flower head. (The flowers can later be given longer stems with additional wire and florist's tape.) Pour an inch or two of the sand or cornmeal mixture into your drying container and settle the flowers on top, leaving some space between the flowers. Slowly add more sand or cornmeal mixture, lifting the petals with a toothpick to ensure that each petal is supported by the mixture. The flowers should be completely covered when you finish.

Flowers with a flat arrangement of petals can be dried with the heads down. Pour an inch or two of the sand or cornmeal mixture into your container and position the flowers so that they do not overlap. Once they are in place, slowly pour in more of the drying medium until the flower heads are completely covered; the stems will stick out of the sand.

Most flowers will dry in three to five weeks, but they can stay in the sand or the cornmeal mixture indefinitely without harm. To check on the drying progress, carefully remove a flower from the container periodically. When the flowers are dry, tilt the container slightly and let the drying medium fall away slowly, or gently scoop the flowers out with a slotted spoon. Dusty residue can be removed from the petals with a watercolor brush. Both the sand and the cornmeal mixture can be used repeatedly, just be sure they are thoroughly dry beforehand.

SILICA-GEL

Drying with a chemical desiccant made from sandlike silica-gel crystals produces the most vivid, natural-color flowers. This method is also fast: silica gel, which actually draws the moisture from petals, dries plants in days rather than weeks. It can be used with many flowers, including orchids and lilies, that become discolored and shriveled when dried by other means.

However, silica gel also has certain drawbacks. Flowers will disintegrate if left in the medium for too long and must be checked regularly during the drying process. Flowers dried in silica gel are also extremely brittle and require careful handling while they are being placed in arrangements. Once dried, the flowers must be kept in conditions with very low humidity, or they will reabsorb moisture and become limp. (Chemical desiccants are also expensive relative to other drying methods.)

Silica gel is available from florists and garden-supply companies, and is used in exactly the same way as the sand and cornmeal mixtures described above. However, the drying must be done in airtight containers, such as cookie tins, to prevent the silica gel from drawing moisture from the air. The drying time is usually two or three days for flowers with a single row of petals, and five to seven days for fuller flowers.

The silica gel can be used repeatedly, but must be dried out each time. Before reuse, pour the crystals into a baking pan and place the pan in a 250° oven for several minutes, until the crystals are fully dried. Store the silica gel in airtight tins between uses.

Dried-Flower Wreath

Wreaths of dried flowers can be enjoyed all year long; they are pretty additions to almost any decor and make welcome gifts. The pastel colors and dainty feeling of the roses, baby's-breath, and other flowers in the wreath opposite give it an old-fashioned country charm. You can, of course, combine plants in a wreath in any way that suits your taste and imagination. You might try making a thematic arrangement, using dried spring flowers perhaps, or mix flowers that have different blooming seasons, using varied colors and sizes. (To learn how to dry your own flowers, see pages 156-157.)

The flowers used in making a wreath can be chosen to convey a particular sentiment or message. Roses, for example, symbolize love, while red and white roses together represent unity. Violets stand for faithfulness, and bluebells constancy. Pansies will tell someone, "I'm thinking of you."

◆ IMPORTANT INFORMATION

The instructions that follow are for the wreath shown here, but they can easily be adapted to a varied choice of flowers, herbs, and leaves. The wreath is assembled on a ready-made straw base that is marked into five equal sections before being covered. Each section is covered with overlapping layers of flowers and leaves that are bound to the straw base with transparent nylon sewing thread (available in the notions department of most variety stores).

Before you arrange the flowers and leaves, you will need to cluster and tape them into small, manageable bunches; refer to the section Preparing the Flowers and Leaves on page 160 to learn how to make the bunches. To arrange the flowers and leaves on each section of the wreath base, refer to the Schematic Diagram on page 161. To achieve the fullness of the wreath shown here, be sure to overlap the bunches generously.

◆ MATERIALS AND EQUIPMENT

Dried materials:
6 stems sea lavender
5 stems baby's-breath
5 stems white statice
25 pink rose blossoms
15 rose-pink carnation blossoms
15 lamb's-ear leaves
5 small or 2 large white hydrangea blossoms
15 stems bunnytail grass
10 stems pink larkspur
10 stems lavender

1 straw wreath base, 12 inches in
    diameter
Transparent nylon sewing thread
Small pruning shears
Wire cutters
2 T-pins
1 roll florist's tape, white or green
Florist's wire
Measuring tape
Black marking pen

◆ PREPARING THE FLOWERS AND LEAVES

Using the pruning shears, cut all the stems about 3 inches below the blossoms or leaves. Make up bunches of flowers as specified below, taping the ends of the stems together for about 2 inches with florist's tape.

Sea lavender (20 bunches): Use three 3-inch-wide clusters per bunch.

Baby's-breath (20 bunches): Use three 3-inch-wide clusters per bunch.

White statice (5 bunches): Use three 3-inch-wide clusters per bunch.

Roses (5 bunches): Use 5 blossoms per bunch.

Carnations (5 bunches): Use 3 blossoms per bunch.

Lamb's-ears (5 bunches): Use 3 leaves per bunch.

Hydrangea (5 bunches): Use one 3-inch-wide blossom per bunch or break apart larger blossoms to make 3-inch-wide bunches.

Bunnytail grass (5 bunches): Use 3 stems per bunch.

Pink larkspur (5 bunches): Use 2 stems per bunch.

Lavender (5 bunches): Use 2 stems per bunch.

◆ DIRECTIONS

1. *Preparing the wreath base:* Pass a piece of florist's wire through the center of the wreath base and wrap it around to the back, twisting it to make a hanging loop. The design of the wreath has no particular top or bottom, so the placement of the loop will not affect the steps that follow. With the marking pen, mark lines on the base to divide it into five equal sections.

2. *Attaching the thread:* Place the base on a worktable with one section centered as if at "twelve o'clock." Push the tip of one T-pin into the base about 2 inches in from the right-hand marking line of this section. With the nylon thread still attached to its spool, wrap the end of the thread around the pin several times, then push the pin completely into the base. Wind the thread several times around base to secure. Place the base on the worktable as before.

3. *Covering the first section of the wreath base:* Referring to the Schematic Diagram opposite, overlap the prepared bunches, positioning them in numerical order. All the heads should point clockwise and be angled toward the inner or outer edges of the wreath base, resulting in all the stems pointing counterclockwise and angling toward the middle of the section (Illustration A). As you work, bind each bunch to the wreath base by wrapping the spool and thread around the base and over the stems several times before positioning the next bunch.

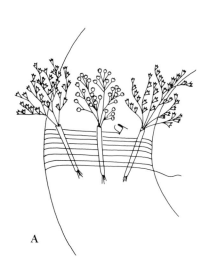

A

4. *Covering the second section of the base:* Attach the flowers and leaves in the same order as in the first section, but reverse the inside/outside positioning of the white statice and the roses (bunches #4 and #5), the carnations and the bunnytail grass (bunches #7 and #13), and the pink larkspur and the lavender (bunches #12 and #16). For example, where in the first section you placed white statice to the outside of the base, in the second section you will angle it to the inside.

5. *Covering the remainder of the base:* Cover the third section in the same manner as the first. Cover the fourth section in the same manner as the second. For the fifth section, judge the placement of the bunches by eye, and try not to duplicate the arrangement that appears in the section on either side. When you reach the beginning of the first section, slide the ends of the stems under the heads of the first-section flowers and bind them carefully so that the thread does not show.

6. *Finishing the wreath:* When the wreath base is completely covered, push the tip of the second T-pin into the base at the end of the last section, wind the thread around it several times, and push the pin into the base. Snip the thread. Look over the finished wreath; if you notice any holes or gaps, make a few more bunches of sea lavender, baby's-breath, lamb's-ears, or bunnytail grass and tuck them in. ◆

Schematic Diagram

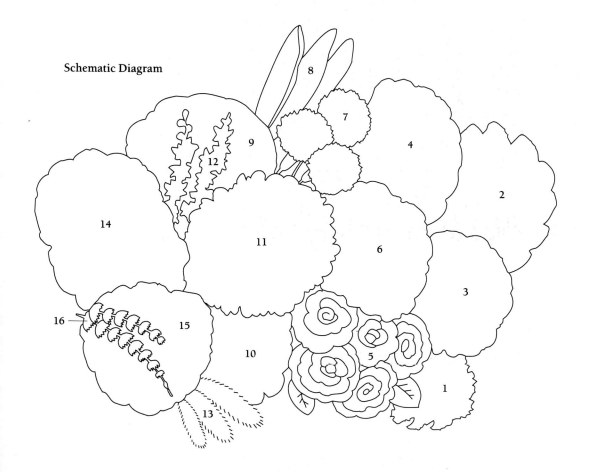

1 · sea lavender

2 · sea lavender

3 · baby's-breath

4 · white statice

5 · roses

6 · baby's-breath

7 · carnations

8 · lamb's-ears

9 · sea lavender

10 · sea lavender

11 · hydrangea

12 · pink larkspur

13 · bunnytail grass

14 · baby's-breath

15 · baby's-breath

16 · lavender

A Country Shelf

Shaker craftsmanship inspired the design of the painted peg-rack shelf opposite. Shaker dwellings were models of cleanliness, and the Shakers themselves devised many ways to make housekeeping efficient. While rooms were typically devoid of moldings or woodwork where dust might settle, peg racks were often mounted on walls so that chairs could be hung out of the way when a room was being swept. (Buckets, bonnets, and tools might also be neatly stored on a peg rack.) The Shaker pegs were unique in design: they were lobed at one end to keep things from sliding off, and threaded at the other so that they could be screwed into the wooden rail or board.

◆ IMPORTANT INFORMATION

This peg-rack shelf is made from two pieces of 1 x 4 pine. Three edges of each piece are beveled, then the two pieces are glued and screwed together. Although it is easiest to bevel the edges with a table saw or router, you can achieve the same effect using a hand plane. After the shelf is assembled, it is painted, then heavily sanded for a timeworn appearance. The Shaker-style pegs can be found at hobby stores or lumberyards.

◆ MATERIALS AND EQUIPMENT

1 piece 1 x 4 pine board, 4 feet long	Wood screws, #6 x 1¾ inches
3 Shaker pegs with ½-inch base	Wood glue
Flat latex paint in white and dark blue	Wood filler
Table saw	Sandpaper, 100 grit
Drill with 7/16- and ⅛-inch bits and	Screwdriver
countersink bit	Hammer
Router or hand plane	Metal straightedge
2-inch flat paintbrush	Paper towels

◆ DIRECTIONS

   1. *Cutting the wood:* Using the table saw, square off one end of the pine board. Using the straightedge and a pencil, measure and mark a line 24 inches in from the square end. Cut on the marked line. Mark this piece "S," for the shelf board. Measure and mark a line 22¾ inches in from the cut end of the remaining board. Cut on the marked line. Mark this piece "P," for the peg board.

   2. *Beveling the boards:* With the table saw set at a 45-degree angle, bevel one long side of the shelf board, leaving the lower ⅛ inch unbeveled. Bevel both short ends of the board in the same manner. Repeat to bevel the peg board.

According to the Shaker Millennial Laws, "Fancy articles of any kind…superfluously finished, trimmed, or ornamented are not suitable for Believers. Whatever is fashioned, let it be plain and simple, unembellished by superfluities which add nothing to its goodness and durability."

3. *Marking the peg placements:* With the beveled side up, place the peg board on a worktable. Measure and mark a line 1½ inches in along the unbeveled edge. Find the middle of this line and mark. Measure along the line and make a mark 7½ inches to either side of the first mark.

4. *Drilling the peg holes:* Using the $\frac{7}{16}$-inch bit, drill a hole $\frac{5}{8}$ inch deep at each of the three marks. Then, using the $\frac{1}{8}$-inch bit, drill the two outer holes all the way through the board.

5. *Marking the shelf board for screws:* With the beveled side up, place the shelf board on the worktable. Measure and mark a line ½ inch in along the unbeveled edge. Find the middle of this line and mark. Measure along the line and make a mark 10 inches to either side of the first mark.

6. *Drilling the screw holes:* Using the $\frac{1}{8}$-inch bit, drill through the shelf board at each mark. Turn the board over and, using the countersink bit, countersink the holes.

7. *Attaching the shelf board to the peg board:* With the beveled side up, place the shelf board on the worktable so that the edge with the screw holes is nearest to you. Apply glue along the top edge of the peg board and center the peg board over the screw holes on the shelf board; the back of the peg board should be flush with the back edge of the shelf board, forming a right angle. Turn the unit over and screw the shelf board to the peg board through the holes, countersinking the screws $\frac{1}{16}$ inch.

8. *Preparing for painting:* Fill the screw holes with the wood filler. Glue a peg into the middle hole. Let the glue and wood filler dry. Sand all the surfaces lightly.

9. *Painting:* Prime the boards and pegs with one coat of white paint. Let dry. Paint the boards and pegs in dark blue. Let dry. Sand through the paint to round all the sharp edges and to give the wood a timeworn appearance.

10. *Mounting:* Screw the shelf to the wall through the outer peg holes, using screws and anchors appropriate to the wall type. Using a scrap of wood or a folded towel to protect the peg heads, carefully tap the remaining pegs into the board with a hammer. ◆

Noah's Ark

From the 1600s to the early 20th century, Noah's ark toys like the one above were among the most popular children's playthings on both sides of the Atlantic. During the 1800s in America, the arks were considered appropriate "Sunday" toys—as instructional as they were fun—that could be played with quietly on the day of rest. While many Noah's ark toys were imported from Europe (entire towns in Germany were devoted to producing arks, animals, and the small figures of Noah and his family), they were also produced in America; some particularly distinctive examples were crafted and painted by woodcarvers in Pennsylvania and New England. Nearly all arks include a deck for the animals and a dove perched on the roof.

◆ IMPORTANT INFORMATION

You will need a table saw to cut the ark, and a band saw or scroll saw to cut the animals. (These are potentially dangerous tools and should only be used by someone who understands how to operate them safely.) The ark is cut out following the Scaled Schematic Diagrams on page 168. The patterns for the animals shown here are full size; you can paint them freehand or trace the details onto them using artist's transfer paper. Use an appropriate-size brush for the area you are painting.

◆ MATERIALS AND EQUIPMENT

1 piece ½-inch pine board, 8 inches x 12 feet

1 piece ¼-inch pine board or plywood, 6 x 12 inches

1 piece wood dowel, ⅛ inch in diameter, 1½ inches long

Acrylic craft paints: 8 ounces each in white, cream, barn red, and black; 2 ounces each in pink, light brown, gold, green, and gray

Wooden kitchen matches

Table saw

Band saw or scroll saw

Drill with ⅛- and 1/16-inch bits

Wire nails, #18 x 1 inch

Assorted flat paintbrushes, ¼ to 2 inches

Small, fine-pointed paintbrush

Tracing paper

Artist's transfer paper (optional)

Wood glue

Wood filler

Putty knife

Hammer

Mat knife

Sandpaper, 100 grit

Masking tape

T-square

Ruler

◆ CUTTING THE ANIMALS

Using a pencil, trace the full-size Animal Patterns opposite onto the tracing paper and cut out. One at a time, place the paper patterns (except for the dove) on the ½-inch pine, draw around them with the pencil, and cut out, using the band saw or scroll saw. (Draw and cut one lion and lioness and one bull and cow; draw and cut two of each of the other animals.) Draw the dove on the ¼-inch pine or plywood and cut out.

ANIMAL PATTERNS

Scaled Schematic Diagrams

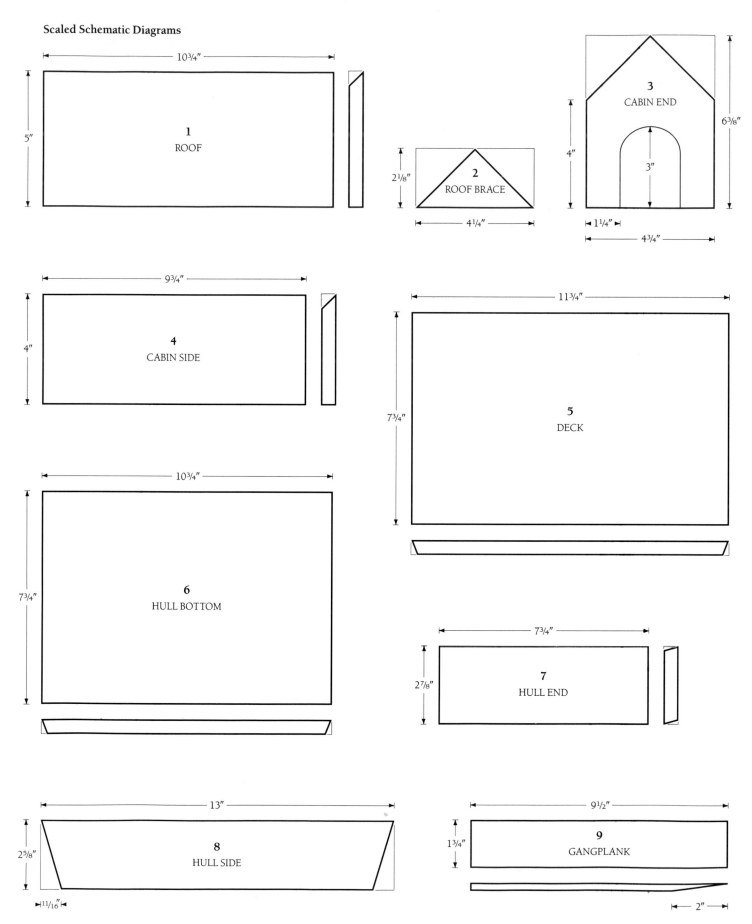

10¾″

5″

1
ROOF

2⅛″

2
ROOF BRACE

4¼″

3
CABIN END

6⅜″

4″

3″

1¼″

4¾″

9¾″

4″

4
CABIN SIDE

11¾″

7¾″

5
DECK

10¾″

7¾″

6
HULL BOTTOM

7¾″

2⅞″

7
HULL END

13″

2⅝″

8
HULL SIDE

11/16″

9½″

1¾″

9
GANGPLANK

2″

◆CUTTING THE ARK

Using the table saw, cut the pieces listed below from the ½-inch pine. Refer to the Scaled Schematic Diagrams opposite for the dimensions. Mark all the pieces with the appropriate number for quick reference. Do not sand any of the pieces.

Roof (*piece #1*): Cut two; on each piece, bevel one long edge at a 45-degree angle.

Roof brace (*piece #2*): Cut two.

Cabin end (*piece #3*): Cut two; in one piece, cut the doorway arch, using the band saw or scroll saw.

Cabin side (*piece #4*): Cut two; on each piece, bevel one long edge at a 45-degree angle.

Deck (*piece #5*): Cut one; bevel each short edge at a 15-degree angle.

Hull bottom (*piece #6*): Cut one; bevel each short edge at a 15-degree angle.

Hull end (*piece #7*): Cut two; on each piece, bevel each long edge at a 15-degree angle.

Hull side (*piece #8*): Cut two.

Cut the following pieces from the ¼-inch pine or plywood:

Gangplank (*piece #9*): Cut one; taper 2 inches at one end.

Gangplank lip: Cut one piece ¼ x ¼ x 1¾ inches.

◆ ASSEMBLING THE ARK

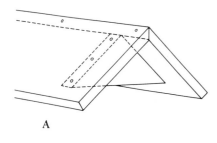

A

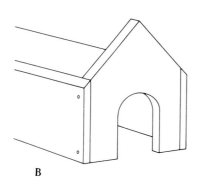

B

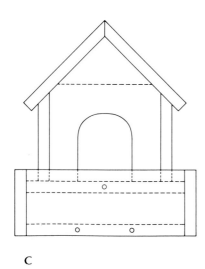

C

1. *Assembling the roof:* Apply glue to the 45-degree edge of each of the roof pieces (pieces #1). Place the glued edges together and secure with four evenly spaced nails. Using the ruler and pencil, make a mark 1⅛ inches in from each end of the peak on the inside of the roof. Apply glue to the 3-inch edges of each of the roof braces (pieces #2). Place one brace to the inside of a mark at the peak and secure with three evenly spaced nails hammered into it through the roof (Illustration A). Repeat to position and secure the second brace.

2. *Assembling the cabin:* Apply glue to the side edges of one cabin end (piece #3). With the beveled edges up, stand both cabin side pieces (pieces #4) on a worktable parallel to each other and insert one cabin end between them so that the edges are flush and square. Secure each corner with a nail hammered from the cabin side into the end (Illustration B). Repeat for the other cabin end. With the beveled side down, place the deck (piece #5) on the worktable. Using the ruler and pencil, draw a rectangle 1 inch in from the edges. Apply glue to the bottom edge of the cabin and position the cabin on the marked rectangle. Secure the cabin to the deck with a nail toenailed (hammered at an angle) through the side of the cabin into the deck at each corner.

3. *Assembling the hull:* Apply glue to the beveled ends of the hull bottom (piece #6) and, with the unbeveled side up, place it on the worktable. Place one hull end (piece #7) against a glued edge so that the bottom edges are flush, and secure with two evenly spaced nails hammered through the end into the bottom. Repeat to attach the other hull end. On one side of the hull, apply glue to the edge of the hull bottom and to the edge of the hull ends. With the edges flush, place one hull side (piece #8) against the glued edges, and secure with seven evenly spaced nails hammered through it into the adjacent pieces. Repeat to attach the other hull side.

4. *Putting the ark together:* Apply glue along all four edges of the deck. Lower it into the hull, making sure that it is level. Secure with a nail hammered through the center of each hull side and end (Illustration C). Using the putty knife, fill all the nail holes with the wood filler. Let it dry, then sand flush with the wood.

5. *Making the gangplank:* Using the ruler and pencil, measure and mark ½-inch intervals across the length of the untapered side of the gangplank (piece #9). Turn it over, and glue the lip across the untapered end; let the glue set for a few minutes. Turn the gangplank over again. Glue a matchstick across it at each pencil mark, and at each end, keeping all the match heads to the same side. Let the glue dry completely. Using the mat knife, cut the match heads off flush with the plank.

6. *Finishing the dove:* Using the ⅛-inch bit, drill a hole in the bottom edge of the dove. Dip one end of the dowel in glue, then insert it into the hole. Using the ruler and pencil, measure and mark a dot on the roof peak 2¾ inches in from one end. Using the ³⁄₁₆-inch bit, drill a hole at the mark, for the placement of the dove.

◆ PAINTING

1. *Priming the ark and animals:* Paint the ark, roof, and gangplank in white. Paint the edges and one side of the animals in white; let dry. Turn them over; paint the other sides. Let all the paint dry completely.

2. *Painting the ark:* Paint the gangplank, the inside of the cabin, the deck, and the inner edge of the rail around the hull in cream; let dry. To protect the deck while painting the cabin exterior, mask it with tape all along the cabin edges. Paint the cabin and the top of the ark rail in barn red. Let dry. Paint the hull and all the roof surfaces in black. With masking tape, outline two 1-inch-square windows on each side of the cabin and paint them in black. Remove all the tape when the paint is dry.

3. *Painting the animals:* Paint the animals as shown in the photograph on page 165; let the background colors dry before painting the details. (If you do not wish to paint the details freehand, slide a small piece of transfer paper, carbon side down, between each pattern and the corresponding animal and trace over the detail on the pattern with a pencil to transfer it to the wooden animal. Reverse the patterns to trace the details onto the other side of the animals.) Let all the paint dry completely.

4. *Sanding the ark and animals:* Sand through the paint to round all sharp edges. To give a well-worn look to the pieces, sand again in areas that would logically receive the most use, such as the doorway, roof, and hull edges. ◆

Credits

CRAFTS (see also PROPS, below): **Cover:** see specific craft projects. **Pages 10-11:** all sewing boxes adapted from a Victorian design and, except velvet box, executed by Linda Mason, The Watermelon Patch, Manhasset, NY. **Pages 23, 30, 38, 39, 44:** all crafts by Linda Mason, The Watermelon Patch, Manhasset, NY. **Page 51:** sampler by The Scarlet Letter, Sullivan, WI. Frames and catalog available. **Pages 58-59:** hand towels adapted and embroidered by Stephanie Gildersleeve, Brooklyn, NY, from a 1930s towel provided by Abby Ruoff, Shady, NY. **Page 65:** Irish-stitch footstool, Rita Klein Needlepoint, NYC. **Pages 68, 69:** Victorian bellpull, Sally Orent, Simply Lace, Huntington, NY. **Pages 76-77:** large oval braided rug by Polly Whitehorn, Great Neck, NY. **Page 82:** hooked rug by Pat Hornafius, Elizabethtown, PA. Catalog and videotape available. **Pages 90, 91:** antique penny rug, Betty Martin Studio, Northport, NY. **Page 97:** cut-and-pierced lampshade designed and executed by Judy Tripp, Mainely Shades, Falmouth, ME. Books available. **Page 100:** scherenschnitt doves by Claudia Hopf, Kennebunk, ME. Books available. **Pages 104-105:** marbled papers by Faith Harrison, East Hampton, MA. Marbling supplies available. **Pages 110-111:** bandboxes by A Touch of Ivy, NYC. Catalog available. **Page 115:** decoupage dresser set by Ginger Schafer Hansen, NYC. **Page 125:** stenciled tablecloth by Marjorie Yoder, Morgantown, PA. **Page 128:** floor cloth by Dee Shapiro, Great Neck, NY; consultants—Nancy Ferrari, Huntington, NY, and Nancy Good Cayford, Amherst, NH. **Pages 134-135:** game board by Dee Shapiro, Great Neck, NY; consultant—Beverly Stessel, Milford, ME. **Pages 140, 142-143:** all grain-painted boxes by Rubens Teles, Jay Johnson's America's Folk Heritage Gallery, NYC, except pale green sponged box behind oval box, page 140, courtesy of Abby Ruoff, Shady, NY. **Page 147:** twig frame by Abby Ruoff, Shady, NY. **Page 150:** bird feeder by Tom Ames, Olde Ways, Forest, VA. **Page 159:** floral wreath by Betsy Williams, A Proper Season, Andover, MA. Catalog available. **Pages 162, 165:** shelf and Noah's ark by Tom Ames, Olde Ways, Forest, VA. **PHOTOGRAPHY:** Cover and pages 10-11, 17, 20-21, 23, 30, 38, 51, 58-59, 65, 68, 69, 90, 97, 110-111, 115, 147, 165: George Ross. Frontispiece and pages 8, 19, 28-29, 42-43, 48, 74, 76-77, 81, 88-89, 94, 100, 104-105, 109, 118, 120-121, 125, 128, 134-135, 140, 142-143, 144, 150, 153, 154-155, 156-157, 159: Steven Mays. Pages 14-15, 102-103, 122-123, 132-133: Stephen Donelian. Pages 39, 44, 82, 91, 162: Rob Whitcomb. Page 56: (top) courtesy of Old Sturbridge Village, Sturbridge, MA, photo by Henry E. Peach; (bottom) courtesy of The Henry Francis duPont Winterthur Museum, Wilmington, DE. Page 57: (top) courtesy of Old Sturbridge Village, photo by Henry E. Peach; (bottom) America Hurrah, NYC. Page 63: courtesy of The Pennsylvania German Society, Birdsboro, PA. Pages 138, 139: Schecter Lee. **ILLUSTRATIONS:** Pages 12, 18, 26, 32, 33, 45, 52, 54-55, 60 (top), 61 (top), 62, 66, 67, 70, 71, 72-73, 78, 79, 86, 92 (left), 148, 152, 170: Patrick J. O'Brien. Pages 22 (left), 40, 41 (top), 98, 107, 108, 112, 113, 131, 160: Ray Skibinski. Pages 13, 22 (right bottom), 25, 27, 34-35, 36-37, 41 (bottom), 46-47, 60-61 (bottom), 85, 87, 92 (bottom), 93, 99, 101, 114, 126-127, 130, 137, 149, 161, 167, 168: computer drawings by Timothy Jeffs. **PROPS** (see also CRAFTS, above): The Editors would like to thank the following for their courtesy in lending items for photography. Items not listed below are privately owned. **Frontispiece:** bandboxes—A Touch of Ivy, NYC; hand towel—Abby Ruoff, Shady, NY. **Page 8:** buttons—Renaissance Buttons, Evanston, IL; fabric—The Watermelon Patch, Manhasset, NY; thimble—Primrose Lane, Manhasset, NY.; needlecase and sewing machine—Sara Bowman. **Pages 10-11:** velvet sewing box—Waltzing Matilda, Huntington, NY; wallcovering, "Rouen," from *Victoria Morland's Through the Looking Glass*—Raintree Designs, Inc., NYC; small thimble case and thimbles—Primrose Lane, Manhasset, NY; basket—Watermelon Patch, Manhasset, NY. **Pages 14-15:** pincushions—Judy Awrylo. **Page 17:** napkins and place mats—Le Jacquard Français from Palais Royal, Charlottesville, VA. **Page 19:** all buttons—Tender Buttons, NYC. **Pages 20-21:** pillow forms—The Company Store, La Crosse, WI; Laura Ashley lace throw pillow—J. P. Stevens, NYC. **Page 23:** pillow—Linda Mason, Manhasset, NY; teddy bear—Anneliese Rapp, NYC; antique bed and chair—Jones Road Antiques, NYC. **Pages 28-29:** fabric, tea-dyed stuffed animals, heart chain—The Watermelon Patch, Manhasset, NY. **Page 30:** wicker chair—Wicker Garden, NYC; pillow and blanket—Sweet Nellie, NYC. **Page 38:** lace pillow—Gear, NYC; coverlet and pillowcases—Laura Fisher/Antique Quilts and Americana, NYC. **Pages 42-43:** topsy-turvy dolls—Elizabeth DeBarto Skinner, Southampton, NY; Mrs. Lenon Hoyte, Aunt Len's Doll and Toy Museum, NYC. **Page 44:** marbles—The Watermelon Patch, Manhasset, NY. **Page 48:** needles and Persian wool—DMC Corp., South Kearny, NJ; thimble and needlecase—Primrose Lane, Manhasset, NY; embroidery hoop—Watermelon Patch, Manhasset, NY; scissors—Sara Bowman; bargello canvas—Zweigart Canvas ® courtesy Joan Toggitt, Ltd., West Caldwell, NJ; **Page 51:** frame—The Scarlet Letter, Sullivan, WI; wallcovering, "Agatha Wade," from the American Collection—Stroheim & Romann, NYC. **Page 63:** hand towels—private collection, courtesy The Pennsylvania German Society, Birdsboro, PA. **Page 74:** covered basket and thread—Watermelon Patch, Manhasset, NY. **Pages 76-77:** braided rugs—Polly Whitehorn, Great Neck, NY; Roslyn House Antiques, Roslyn, NY; ABC Carpet, NYC. **Page 82:** table, hogscraper candlesticks, painted Shaker box—Roslyn House Antiques, Roslyn, NY; candles—Candlewick, Portland, MI. **Pages 88-89:** Grenfell mats, rugs, purse—Mr. and Mrs. Robert Meltzer,

NYC. **Page 90**: candles—Candlewick, Portland, MI. **Page 94**: wallpaper and bandboxes—A Touch of Ivy, NYC. **Page 97**: lamp base—Judy Tripp, Mainely Shades, Falmouth, ME. **Page 100**: painted scherenschnitt—Claudia Hopf, courtesy of The Watermelon Patch, Manhasset, NY. **Pages 102-103**: all papers—New York Central Art Supply, NYC. **Pages 104-105**: marbleized paper and supplies—Faith Harrison, East Hampton, MA; enamel pitcher—Bonnie Slotnick, NYC. **Page 109**: marbleized papers—Faith Harrison. **Page 118**: brushes—Winsor & Newton, Secaucus, NJ; also available at New York Central Art Supply, NYC. **Pages 120-121**: paintbrushes, acrylic artists' colors—Binney & Smith, Inc., Easton, PA; japan paints—H. Behlen & Bros., Amsterdam, NY; alkyd and oil art-

ists' colors, palette, palette knife, cup—Winsor & Newton, Secaucus, NJ; paints and accessories also available at New York Central Art Supply, NYC. **Pages 122-123**: fans, liners, rounds, brights—Winsor & Newton, Secaucus, NJ; also available at New York Central Art Supply; badger softener, overgrainer, stippler—Whistler Collection; stencil and sponge brushes—New York Central Art Supply, NYC. **Page 128**: painted cupboard—made by John Dossett and painted by Weldine Dossett, Campbelltown, PA. **Pages 132-133**: handcrafted floor cloths, top row: Philadelphia Floorcloths, Inc., Narbeth, PA; second row, all: Good & Co. Floorclothmakers, Amherst, NH; third row, all but third from left: Philadelphia Floorcloths; third from left: Good & Co.; fourth row, left: Philadel-

phia Floorcloths; right: Good & Co.; bottom row: Good & Co. **Page 144**: wreath form and dried flowers—Betsy Williams, A Proper Season, Andover, MA; dried flowers—Primrose Lane, Manhasset, NY; tin box—Bonnie Slotnick, NYC. **Page 147**: Pendleton blanket—Laura Fisher/Antique Quilts & Americana, NYC. **Page 153**: selected seeds, cracked corn, peanut hearts—Duncraft, Pencook, NH. **Pages 154-157**: folding drying rack, #25-333088—Gardener's Eden catalog, San Francisco, CA; all dried flowers—Galerie Felix Flower, NYC. **Page 162**: wallcovering, "Burnett," #5563, from Designers Signature Collection—Greeff Fabrics, Garden City, NY; rag balls, basket, apron—Kathy Wilson, Apple Valley, MN. **Page 165**: table runner—The Watermelon Patch, Manhasset, NY.

Index

Acknowledgments

Our thanks to Sara Bowman, Nancy Good Cayford, Weldine and John Dossett, Jane Fitzpatrick, Stephanie Gildersleeve, Susan and Jack Hale, Claudia and Carroll Hopf, Pat Hornafius, Carter G. Houck, Christina and Michael Kearney, Paula Laverty, Linda Lefko, Karen Marton, Linda Mason, Barbara Meltzer, Frances Beck Reynolds, Eleanor Schrumm, Jeanne Shapiro, Gloria Shattil, Carol Spier, Donna and Peter Steffen, Steve Steinberg, The Watermelon Patch, Frederick Weiser, and Ivy Weitzman for their help on this book.

First printing
Published simultaneously in Canada
School and library distribution by Silver Burdett Company,
Morristown, New Jersey

TIME-LIFE is a trademark of Time Incorporated U.S.A.

Production by Giga Communications, Inc.
Printed in U.S.A.

Library of Congress Cataloging-in-Publication Data

Country crafts. (American country)
Includes index.
1. Handicraft—United States.
I. Time-Life Books.   II. Series.
TT23.C67   1989   745.5   89.4638
ISBN 0-8094-6770-4
ISBN 0-8094-6771-2 (lib. bdg.)

American Country was created by Rebus, Inc., and published by Time-Life Books.

REBUS, INC.

Publisher: RODNEY FRIEDMAN • Editor: MARYA DALRYMPLE
Executive Editor: RACHEL D. CARLEY • Managing Editor: BRENDA SAVARD • Consulting Editor: CHARLES L. MEE, JR.
Associate Editor: SARA COLLINS MEDINA • Copy Editors: ALEXA BARRE, HELEN SCOTT-HARMAN
Writers: JUDITH CRESSY, ROSEMARY G. RENNICKE
Design Editors: NANCY MERNIT, CATHRYN SCHWING
Test Kitchen Director: GRACE YOUNG • Editor, The Country Letter: BONNIE J. SLOTNICK
Editorial Assistants: SANTHA CASSELL, LEE CUTRONE • Contributing Editor: ANNE MOFFAT
Indexer: MARILYN FLAIG

Art Director: JUDITH HENRY • Associate Art Director: SARA REYNOLDS
Designers: AMY BERNIKER, TIMOTHY JEFFS
Photographer: STEVEN MAYS • Photo Editor: SUE ISRAEL
Photo Assistant: ROB WHITCOMB • Freelance Photographers: STEPHEN DONELIAN, GEORGE ROSS
Freelance Photo Stylists: VALORIE FISHER, DEE SHAPIRO

Series Consultants: BOB CAHN, HELAINE W. FENDELMAN, LINDA C. FRANKLIN, GLORIA GALE,
KATHLEEN EAGEN JOHNSON, JUNE SPRIGG, CLAIRE WHITCOMB

Time-Life Books Inc. is a wholly owned subsidiary of TIME INCORPORATED.

Editor-in-Chief: JASON McMANUS • Chairman and Chief Executive Officer: J. RICHARD MUNRO
President and Chief Operating Officer: N. J. NICHOLAS JR. • Editorial Director: RICHARD B. STOLLEY

THE TIME INC. BOOK COMPANY

President and Chief Executive Officer: KELSO F. SUTTON
President, Time Inc. Books Direct: CHRISTOPHER T. LINEN

TIME-LIFE BOOKS INC.

Editor: GEORGE CONSTABLE • Executive Editor: ELLEN PHILLIPS
Director of Design: LOUIS KLEIN • Director of Editorial Resources: PHYLLIS K. WISE
Editorial Board: RUSSELL B. ADAMS JR., DALE M. BROWN, ROBERTA CONLAN, THOMAS H. FLAHERTY,
LEE HASSIG, DONIA ANN STEELE, ROSALIND STUBENBERG
Director of Photography and Research: JOHN CONRAD WEISER
Assistant Director of Editorial Resources: ELISE RITTER GIBSON

President: JOHN M. FAHEY JR.
Senior Vice Presidents: ROBERT M. DeSENA, JAMES L. MERCER, PAUL R. STEWART, JOSEPH J. WARD
Vice Presidents: STEPHEN L. BAIR, STEPHEN L. GOLDSTEIN, JUANITA T. JAMES,
ANDREW P. KAPLAN, CAROL KAPLAN, SUSAN J. MARUYAMA, ROBERT H. SMITH
Supervisor of Quality Control: JAMES KING
Publisher: JOSEPH J. WARD

For information about any Time-Life book please call 1-800-621-7026, or write:
Reader Information, Time-Life Customer Service
P.O. Box C-32068, Richmond, Virginia 23261-2068

Time-Life Books Inc. offers a wide range of fine recordings, including a Rock 'n' Roll Era series.
For subscription information, call 1-800-621-7026, or write TIME-LIFE MUSIC,
P.O. Box C-32068, Richmond, Virginia 23261-2068.